Withdrawn

The Ancient Shore

The

ANCIENT
SHORE

Dispatches from Naples

SHIRLEY HAZZARD
AND FRANCIS STEEGMULLER

THE UNIVERSITY OF CHICAGO PRESS   *Chicago and London*

Shirley Hazzard is the author of six novels, including *The Transit of Venus* (1980, winner of the National Book Critics Circle Award) and *The Great Fire* (2003, winner of the National Book Award). **Francis Steegmuller** (1906–1994), recipient of many awards, was renowned for his translations, editions, and critical studies of Flaubert, and was also the author of numerous biographies, works of nonfiction, and several novels. He and Hazzard were married in 1963 and divided their time between New York, France, and Italy.

The University of Chicago Press, Chicago 60637
The University of Chicago Press, Ltd., London
© 2008 by Shirley Hazzard
All rights reserved. Published 2008
Printed in the United States of America

Portions of this work originally appeared in the following: *House and Gardens*, *Lincoln Center Theater Review*, *The New York Times*, *The New York Times Magazine*, *The New Yorker*, and *The Wall Street Journal*.

17 16 15 14 13 12 11 10 09 08   1 2 3 4 5

ISBN-13: 978-0-226-32201-8 (cloth)
ISBN-10: 0-226-32201-7 (cloth)

Library of Congress Cataloging-in-Publication Data
Hazzard, Shirley, 1931–
    The ancient shore : dispatches from Naples / Shirley Hazzard and Francis Steegmuller.
        p. cm.
    ISBN-13: 978-0-226-32201-8 (cloth : alk. paper)
    ISBN-10: 0-226-32201-7 (cloth : alk. paper) 1. Naples (Italy)—Description and travel. 2. Naples (Italy)—Social life and customs. 3. Naples (Italy)—Civilization. I. Steegmuller, Francis, 1906–1994. Incident at Naples. II. Title. III. Title: Incident at Naples.
    DG844.2.H39 2008
    945'.731—dc22
                                                        2008015420

♾ The paper used in this publication meets the minimum requirements of the American National Standard for Information Sciences—Permanence of Paper for Printed Library Materials, ANSI Z39.48-1992.

CONTENTS

ITALIAN HOURS *Shirley Hazzard*

OF THE MILLIONS who visit Italy each year, some thousands will return there "to live"—to spend a season or a year or two. Of these, a few will remain all their lives. If they are painters, writers, or musicians, they will carry on their trade in an ambiance that still esteems the individual effort of art. If they are scholars, they must take their chances in the gladiatorial arena of Italian erudition. Others may develop a career or, more usually, eke out a living with expatriate odd jobs. And there are some who can afford idleness in that peninsula where the cult of leisure flourishes still and where variety and pleasure can fill up many, though not all, days. No longer visitors, never to be natives, these people have arrived without the grim compulsions of migrants or refugees, and they move for the most part easily through the Italian dance, with excursions to their homeland. For a measure of affluence takes, these days, the edge off finality's blade, and mobility suggests—delusively—that every journey is potentially a round trip.

Those of us who, when young, chose "to live" in the Italy of the postwar decades felt we were doing just that: living more completely among the scenes and sentiments of a humanism the New World could not provide. The Italian admixture of immediacy and continuity, of the long perspective and the intensely personal, was then reasserting itself after years of eclipse. It was a time not of affluence but of renewal, and Italy again offered to travelers her antique genius for human relations—a tact, an expansiveness never quite without form. One was drawn, too, by beauty that owed as much to centuried endurance as to the luminosity of art and that seemed, then, to create an equilibrium as lasting as nature's. Like the historian Jakob Burckhardt, we felt all this was ours "by right of admiration."

I was warned—as are all who pursue their dream—by those who define reality as a sequence of salutary disappointments that "reality" would soon set in. I was reminded that immemorial outsiders had followed that same cisalpine path. Yet we trusted to the private revelation. Of her time in Rome, Elizabeth Bowen wrote: "If my discoveries are other people's commonplaces I cannot help it—for me they retain a momentous freshness." And so, for most of us, it was and is.

I was fortunate when I first lived in Italy in being obliged to work for a year in Naples, a city that in its postwar dereliction had been virtually erased from the modern travel itinerary as arcane and insalubrious (and that for the same reasons remains little touched by tourism today—the last great Italian city whose monuments retain their animate, authentic context). In an old seaside house, nineteenth-century, Pompeian red, I had high, humid rooms and a view that swept the bay—city and volcano, the long Sorrentine cape, and the island of Capri, which floated far or near according to the light. No expatriate English-speaking network existed to modify my ardor or palliate hard lessons. Then in my early twenties, I had lived around the world but had never previously seen Italy, never been there as a footloose tourist, and thus had no adjustment to make. To visit a beautiful country on holiday is a freedom, a suspension. To reside and work there is a commitment for which one must not only forfeit much of the indulgence that Italy extends to visitors but subdue, also, the visitor in oneself.

From other loved Italian places, the bay of Naples drew me back—to white rooms on Capri long ago and also, of recent years, to another seabound house on the Neapolitan shore. My worktable faced a blank wall, for the sights of Siren Land are no aid to concentration. Even so, throughout the day my husband and I would call one another—to see the light on Vesuvius, the red ship, the colored sails, the fishermen hauling nets, and the waves breaking over Roman walls.

The "reality" prefigured to me, like a spread of wet cement, never did "set in." But by definition a leap through the looking glass disturbs one's self-image, and I had to learn something of my own ignorance. Intimacy with another country is ripened by pleasures but also by loneliness and error. It is nurtured through long wet winters as well as radiant days and through the fluctuations of mood inevitable to any strong attachment. The colorful scene will not compensate indefinitely for a sense of exclusion from the exchange of thought and wit. The early hospitality of the Italian tongue in daily matters is little preparation for its exigency in the expression of ideas, and the outsider genially praised for his declarative sentences cannot suspect that years may pass before this elusive language becomes as flexible and spontaneous as his own. The many resident foreigners who remain visitors forever, hovering eternally at a rim, have recoiled from these rigors and may applaud Italian joys or deplore Italian ills, themselves being responsible for neither. Yet a life without responsibility can pall, and most such people will go home at last, having exhausted not Italy but their own capacity for aimlessness.

In Italy we learn, as W. H. Auden noted, "That surfaces need not be superficial / Nor gestures vulgar" and that, since Italian life is to some extent a performance—an idea of the self played out with style—responsiveness and good manners do not guarantee depth and consistency. We learn, too, that the ability to rise to the moment, to the human occasion, is linked to a sense of mortality intrinsic, in Italy, to all that pleases us.

Life in Italy is seldom simple. One does not go there for simplicity but for interest: to make the adventure of existence more vivid, more poignant. I have known that country through dire as well as golden times and have dwelt in town and country, north and south. Whether I wake these mornings in Naples to the Mediterranean lapping the seawall or on Capri to the sight of a nobly indifferent mountain, it is never without realizing, in surprise and gratitude, that it all came to pass and that I—like Goethe, like Byron—am living in Italy.

PART I *Shirley Hazzard*

PILGRIMAGE

WHEN I WAS FIFTEEN, we went to live in the Far East. Was that a pilgrimage—or merely a stroke of great good fortune? It was a destination that I had not sought, and in that way it was more like destiny. Still, there had been, always, the yearning to cross the seas, to know the world: the accessibility to pilgrimage. My childhood had been spent in Australia—a remote, philistine country in those years, and very much a male country, dominated by a defiant masculinity that repudiated the arts. Even in a large, busy city like Sydney, there was little music, there were few museums. There was natural beauty, but almost no visual culture, and even a wide antipathy to painting and painters. What we did have was literature, which came through our British forebears. It was in reading that one could truly live: in one's mind, in books, in the world. A form of pilgrimage.

I traveled to Asia because my father was appointed there. We went first to Japan, and then to live in Hong

Kong for two years. Thus I went by chance to live in one of the most interesting and romantic places in the world, before its city center became a money market and a thicket of skyscrapers. Hong Kong at that time was a last authentic glimpse of empire as it had been—a last glimmering of the Conradian ports, the Conradian islands. The convulsion of the Second World War was just subsiding, there was civil war in China. All Asia was in a state of seething change. When one is young, one accepts that backdrop, engrossed in one's own impressions and events, in one's own destiny. Those years and experiences have haunted me, with their accidental revelations. The contemporary Western world, grappled to its explanations, sets itself to ignore the accidental quality of our existence. For the expression of chance mysteries, we must turn to literature, to art.

Life, for me, has been a succession of such destined accidents, when what was latent in the reading mind and in the aroused imagination acquired reality in daily life. Thus one wasn't completely unprepared for extraordinary places, unpredictable events. The variety and interest of existence had struck us, through literature, as being more real than our factual origins. It was thus that pilgrimage had been set in motion.

My sister contracted tuberculosis in China, and we couldn't remain in that climate. Leaving there was a terrible parting for me. The next destination was New Zealand, again for my father's work. Since then, Australia, New Zealand—

the Antipodes—have greatly changed. Distance itself has diminished with jet travel and with the relative prosperity that allows many of us to move around the world. In those postwar years, however, New Zealand seemed, at least to me, the opposite of a pilgrimage; it seemed as far as possible from where I intended to be. Those islands appeared, then, to exist within an immemorial silence as far as the world was concerned. It was, again, in books that one discovered affinity, event, extension. The city of Wellington had a handful of good small bookshops. I used to buy volumes of poets in the Faber series: new poems from Auden, MacNeice, and their contemporaries; anthologies of young British poets who had died in or survived the Second World War; and Penguins with orange covers. I found a slim volume of new translations by John Heath-Stubbs of the Italian Romantic poet Leopardi, and felt that I had to read these in the original. Far—far as could be—from Italy, I took Italian lessons.

I went to England with my parents. That was an outright pilgrimage, it had long been a dream. In London, as it was then, I could willingly have stayed forever. Destiny intervened, and we came to New York. I applied to the United Nations, and was put in the dungeons there, where I remained some years.

In 1956, because of events in the Middle East, the United Nations opened a temporary staging area at Naples. Due to my Italian lessons in the Antipodes, I was sent for a year to the city that would become part of my life ever after. Destiny, but also pilgrimage: some part of me had been working towards transformation.

I think of a beautiful poem from the 1940s by Henry Reed, called "A Map of Verona." Prevented by war from traveling to an Italian city that filled his thoughts, the poet visits it on a map, without reality—

> . . . Yet you are there, and one day I shall go.
> The train will bring me perhaps in utter darkness,
> And drop me where you are blooming unaware
> That a stranger has entered your gates at last,
> And a new devotion is about to attend and haunt you
> everywhere.

In those lines there is still the ancient nature of pilgrimage: the difficulty, the long yearning; the constancy, the consummation. Arrival as an achievement that cannot be denied—arrival, with all its consequences of transformations, encounters, self-knowledge, exposures, disappointments. The destination is not in this case a sacred shrine, yet it has a magnetic quality and is both a completion and a beginning. In my Australian childhood, the dream was England: six weeks by ship to reach the goal, six weeks to return. A consecration of many months, perhaps a year. People did this once in their lives, but felt that they could die happier having accomplished it. We would see friends off on those departing ships, with such food hampers, such flowers and streamers; such envy.

So many versions of pilgrimage in the world. The holy pilgrimages, to Rome, to Mecca, to the sacred sites of ancient Greece. Novelists and poets are full of pilgrimage. In *War and Peace*, Prince Andrei's pious young sister secretly dreams of making a devout journey to holy shrines, imagining her pure bliss, even if she dies on the way. There is the pilgrimage to lost love, lost youth, such as Thomas Hardy made to the west of England after his first wife's death: a resurrection of emotions that produced, in him, some of the great poems in our language. There can be the journey to reconciliation, the need to revisit the past or to exorcise it.

In all such journeys, Italy looms large. For northerners, for Asians, for Antipodeans, for Americans, Italy, with all its changes, remains a goal: a realization and a reprieve. "God owed me Italy," said the classical archaeologist Wincklemann in the eighteenth century, "for I had suffered so much in my youth." Goethe enters Rome with relief and joy: "All the dreams of my youth have come to life . . . Everything is as I imagined it, yet everything is new." Dr. Johnson, never able to make the pilgrimage, remained aware of the lack. For the historian Burckhardt, the vitality of rich civilization was, even for foreigners, a homecoming: "It was ours by right of admiration." Those past travelers knew much solitude, silence, inconvenience. Even for the most ribald of them—Byron, Flaubert—the experience was in some measure spiritual, touching inmost things, precipitating humility, knowledge, and change. Modern visitors come in haste, in crowds. Jaunts are not pilgrimage. Destiny has no time to set her wheels in motion. Even so, since there has been a goal, there can be revelation.

————◄○►————

"We change our skies, not our souls," Horace cautions. Some souls nevertheless bring with them a capacity for joy, an accessibility to other thoughts and tastes, an ear for other tongues, an eye for other beauty: a readiness. Revelation—so inalienable an element of travel that there is even a luggage of the name—takes multiple and often inward forms. Many a traveler departs in the hope of defining an elusive self or mislaying a burdensome one, of being literally carried away. Literature has prepared us to expect the release of new aspects of ourselves in the presence of the fabled and unfamiliar. Simply by looking on given scenes and monuments human beings have been known to become happier and wiser. Travel is an elixir, a talisman: a spell cast by what has long and greatly been, over what briefly and simply is.

Travel, according to the nineteenth-century French wayfarer Astolphe de Custine, is a means of visiting other centuries. Imagination goes with us on our journey, a thrilling and often beautiful companion. Modern purposefulness gives place to plurality of sensation; explanation is shamed—if not always silenced—by mystery. The traveler simultaneously sheds and receives, and in the very thick of the crowd may still experience the poignant reciprocity of place and person. Even the tourist who only glimpses, from a sealed bus, the Eiffel Tower or the Colosseum, seeks his particle of the holy relic of the world's experience. And how much passion and event have been invested in those famous sights that they should continue to yield meaning—even to the millionth and most casual eye—with unstinted generosity; assimilating decay itself as an enrichment. (A skeptical young woman of Henry James's invention, who supposes Rome to be spoiled, receives the experienced answer: "I think not. It has been spoiled so often.")

Thus the world exchanges, annually, its store of contrasts, adventure, and refreshment, and almost everyone continues to feel the better for it. That the contrasts are dwindling, that adventure is often frenzied, that the modern onslaught of curiosity may itself be depleting the world's reserves of human interest—these are menaces put out of mind along with other presentiments of Armageddon. The great theater that Europe has come to constitute for tourists remains a magnet, though the summer show may sometimes offer standing room only. In the Pacific, the prophecies of Herman Melville and Victor Segalen have been fulfilled at Waikiki; and even the farthest archipelagoes:

> . . . the satiate year impends
> When, wearying of routine-resorts,
> The pleasure-hunter shall break loose, Ned,
> for our Pantheistic ports . . .

Despite such evidence, and the airport bookstall's terse announcement that "Civilization is now in paperback," the exhaustion of travel's immemorial repository of delights is apparently as unthinkable as the extinction of fossil fuels. The very precariousness and anonymity of contemporary existence and its acceleration of destruction and change create a compulsion to seize the moment. The excursion to other centuries—undertaken these days with antibiotics, credit cards, and a return ticket to the twenty-first century—has new urgency and a tinge of valediction. The modern visitor to the past may yet embrace abroad what is déclassé at home—ripeness, grace, ceremony, repose, an acceptance of mortality: waning concepts that may never revisit our planet; while the denizens of ancient places seek, in turn, in newer nations, expansiveness, volatility, an unconcern for and even repudiation of experience. And still others take to the wilderness, for respite from all manifestations of their fellow man. Although the intention of travel is far from noncommittal, its commitment is luxuriously selective: relieved of responsibility for the failings he encounters, the traveler may still enjoy the haunting quality of the antique without its terror; the poetic emanation of past strivings without their anguish; the energy of the future without its aridity. A condition of the attraction of the unknown is that it remain, in some measure, inscrutable.

The coast of my native land supplied, in my case, a first glimpse of the unknown: in the lights—seen from a deck on the first night of sailing to the Orient—of Australian seaboard towns that lay beyond the range of my landlocked childhood excursions. Those clustered lights gave the first sensation of passing a barrier; they were at once departure and discovery. The five-week journey from Sydney to Japan—in a little, old, durable ship that made one brief stop, in a jungle cove of New Guinea, for water—was a fitting preparation for momentous change. Awakening one dawn of befogged vermilion in the Inland Sea of Japan, we were faithfully brought to port, and other travels began. I had read Conrad's "Youth," and lived, in the moment, the closing fragment of that story—waking to the East "so old, so mysterious, resplendent and somber, living and unchanged, full of danger and promise."

That East is unchanged no longer, and such rapture is itself said to come only once. In fact I have reexperienced it many times—spending a moonlit night on deck to sight the coast of Crete, the straits of Messina, the cone of Stromboli; setting foot on an oblivious Europe at Marseilles one September morning; lying off the Cornish coast at sunrise and driving at noon into London through a shambles of blitzed docks. And landing, years later, at Rome one evening in early winter— to mild air, trees in leaf, and baskets of violets for sale on the then unlittered and unsullied Spanish Steps. I remember a snowbound Epiphany in hills south of Florence; blue shutters opening, near Carthage, on a turquoise sea; a hillside of narcissus at Volubilis; the dry summer grass of the Camargue.

Distant lights have retained their power. Time after time, during the transatlantic flight, I have looked out, before sunrise, for the lamps of fishing fleets off Ireland—signals of a life older than memory, perceived from the age of jet propulsion.

I, too, have visited other centuries—in Arcadia itself, in sun-baked towns south of the Atlas and under the colonial arcades of a vanished Hong Kong; I have seen old Chinese women hobble on the stumps of their bound feet, and the scholars passing, gowned and slippered, along the streets of Asia. I have shared, from Monticello, the eighteenth-century vision of America. I have watched French missionary nuns, in white and blue, red parasols aloft above their towering medieval headdress, move unconcerned through tropical rain; and country women, in ceremonial bodices and long dark skirts, stroll down the quays of Venice.

It is women, more usually, who bear such emblems into other times—as, last summer at the port of Capri, a trio of handsome matriarchs who stepped ashore from Catanzaro, gold and silver lace over their coiled hair and on their dresses of rosso antico that swept the ground. By their festive costume they honored the great occasion of travel: Their restraint, among the modern hubbub, was a form of authority, a stately humility before the wonders of this world.

If, on our travels, we are not precisely surprised by such apparitions, such enchantments, it is because we always dreamed we might see them.

The traveler equipped with even one introduction arrives with a card to play, a possible clue to the mystery. Yet those who have never experienced solitude in a strange and complex place—never arrived in the unknown without credentials, without introductions to the right people, or the wrong ones—have missed an exigent luxury. Never to have made the lonely walk along the Seine or Lungarno, or passed those austere evenings on which all the world but oneself has destination and companion, is perhaps never to have felt the full presence of the unfamiliar. It is thus one achieves a slow, indelible intimacy with place, learning to match its moods with one's own. At such times it is as if a destination had awaited us with nearly human expectation and with an exquisite blend of receptivity and detachment.

The moment comes: we intersect a history, a long existence, offering it our fresh discovery as regeneration.

A SCENE OF
ANCIENT FAME

I AM STANDING on a terrace in Naples, on the headland
called Posillipo, looking at the bay. To my left, through umbrella pines, the city—red, ocher, and a centuried sepia—
forms a crescent toward Vesuvius. The volcano, in turn,
sweeps down to the long arc of the Sorrentine peninsula,
which, constituting the southern arm of this gulf, faces me
across a few miles of water—clear enough, in today's pure
light, to distinguish towns and villages and the old tower at
the tip of Cape Minerva, where, in past ages, a great bell was
rung to give warning of Saracen ships. On the right, in the
open sea, Capri and its mountain lie at the horizon. Such
clarity can last for days or announce a sudden storm; and
there are times when the south wind, the humid sirocco,
droops its curtain of warm wool over all the incomparable
scene.

In the past hour, water traffic has consisted of an outgoing tanker loaded to the scuppers, a container ship stacked with big brown blocks, a cruise ship painted blue, two hydrofoils loudly bound for the island of Ischia, and a white ferry returning from Capri. Immediately below me, close to shore, there is a scattering of traditional Neapolitan fishing boats with worn indigo hulls, sometimes under the power of erratic motor, more often silently propelled by the standing man at the oars, whose partner casts or retrieves the net. On fine nights, such boats use lamps to attract the fish that come—said Shelley in Italy—"to worship the delusive flame."

Terse words in dialect then rise to us in darkness and, once in a while, the rhythmic slapping of a paddle used to scare schools of tiny fish—sardines, anchovies—into the net. Fishing from small open boats is the old, hard life of these waters, plied without interruption since this shore was a Roman resort and its sea—none too clean this morning—so thick with the detritus of grandiose new houses that, according to Horace, even the fish complained.

Trawlers also pass here, their catch escorted by flocks of gulls. These larger boats come from as far as Sardinia seeking varieties of bass and grouper—and the bream called orata associated with a Roman entrepreneur, C. Sergius Orata, whose innovative fishponds and oyster beds at nearby Baia attracted the attention of Cicero two thousand years ago. (In his invaluable *Romans on the Bay of Naples*, the classicist John D'Arms observes that Orata, who supplied luxurious equipment to villas along this coast, "was the first Campanian speculator to cater to the leisure of the great grandees." His successors today are legion.)

A regatta of small yachts with colored spinnakers has glided by. Far out, there is a ketch with reefed sails making south, for Amalfi or Salerno. And a huge old three-master, her canvas furled, has left the port of Naples for southern France; with her long bowsprit and the mighty masts that justify their Italian name *alberi*—"trees"—she has, even under engine, the spectral composure of old barks that move as if unmanned and self-aware.

Not far from land, but in deep water, the wave rises and withdraws over a reef capped by an outcropping known as the Salt Rock, the Pietra Salata. At Naples, things are seldom what they seem; and the reef, the rock, are in fact remnants of Roman structures gradually submerged by coastal change. When summer comes, the Roman reef will be active with young swimmers who, coming out from the city in boats and rubber dinghies, use it as a diving board. On warm weekends, the hydrofoils for the islands—for Capri, Procida, Ischia, and even Ponza—pass here constantly; and, late on summer Sundays, this stretch of sea along Posillipo becomes an autostrada of ferries, motor cruisers, and small craft streaming back to Naples. By nightfall, the churning subsides. A few fishermen return, looking for *totano*, the seasonal squid. An old motorboat with colored lights takes families out to dine at the nearby cove of Marechiaro. The measured sound of ocean resumes on the sea wall. There is the turning, barely audible, of the negligible tide.

Now, however, as the wave recedes from the Salt Rock, divisions of stone foundations can for a moment be seen, heavy set, abraded, and purple with encrusted mussels. Ruins of the kind are plentiful round the Neapolitan coast, both above and below water—arches, porches, parapets, the enclosures of ancient baths, docks, fisheries. Farther out on this promontory, there are extensive remains of the Roman villa called *Pausilypon*—in Greek, "a pause from care"—that gave name and fame to the entire headland of Posillipo. A complex of pleasure buildings constructed in the first century BC, during the reign of Augustus, Pausilypon was sumptuous even by standards of the place and era. The villa was left by Vedius Pollio, its cruel and wealthy owner, to Augustus himself—a prudently announced intention that possibly saved Pollio from the hard consequences of imperial envy in his lifetime. Augustus was entertained here—notably, on an occasion when Pollio ordered that a slave who had broken a goblet at table be fed to a tankful of carnivorous eels. Having remonstrated at first in vain, the emperor smashed the rest of the costly dishes and invited the host to impose the same penalty on his sovereign. All told, one feels, not a successful party.

Men are no longer fed to eels here; in fact, quite the contrary. But the old villas that stand out today all along the Posillipo shore are descendants of those Roman palaces—the *villae maritimae*—depicted, with their seaside colonnades, in Vesuvian frescoes. Painted views of Posillipo from the seventeenth and eighteenth centuries illustrate the amazing continuity of a waterfront long bordered with great houses—quite densely, near the small port of Mergellina that marks the juncture of Posillipo with the city proper; quite sparsely, farther out. Until 1812, when Napoleon's deputed "King of Naples," the colorful Joachim Murat, inaugurated the panoramic hillside road of Via di Posillipo, those seaside villas were—like their Roman predecessors—dependent on access by boat (and are best seen by boat today). Long thereafter, when Via Posillipo, as it is known now, was itself lined with pastel palazzi for much of its length, the headland maintained a rural identity: stands of pine and ilex and groves of olive continued to cover its slopes; orchards and vineyards were cultivated above and below the ribbon road of new houses. For Naples, Posillipo—subject of innumerable painted "views" in gouache; much sung, as "Pusilleco," in dialect—remained a visible and visitable paradise, a serene counterpart to the volcano on the opposite side of the bay: a pause, if only a pause, from care.

When, during World War II, Naples was bombarded, Vesuvius erupted, and the Allied front inched northward, with grim suffering, to Monte Cassino, Posillipo—at a short distance from the city's heart—remained a safe haven. Monarchs, generals, statesmen were billeted on the farthest of the great Posillipo properties: Winston Churchill cruised about the harbor from Villa Rivalta; the vacillating king of Italy fished from a cockleshell off Villa Rosebery; and a sergeant from Ohio scratched his name into the terrace tiles at Villa Barracco—where King George VI was also a wartime guest. Naples absorbs the exotic easily—having, even to excess, the gift of taking strangeness for granted and balking only at system. The host of Allied troops, departing, gave place to the emissaries of NATO—who furnished, with all the wonders of the PX, their modern apartments in blocks newly pitched on the Posillipo hill.

When I first came to Naples in the 1950s and lived for a year at Posillipo, in a red, romantic house that rises from the sea on Roman foundations, this district was still recognizably close to the scene of past centuries—not only in appearance, but in its expansive relation to the intensity of the city. Naples then was a blitzed town of large-eyed, overburdened, resilient people. Many of its great churches and palaces lay open to the elements; its waterfront was a shambles. To drive out from the shattered city after work to the colors and flowers of Posillipo and old walls hung with plumbago, bougainvillea, and jasmine; to swim from inlets and grottoes of the blond tuff of which this cape is composed; to watch, from any balcony or shop front or curve of Via Posillipo, the unfolding light and adventure of the bay, was to achieve tranquility without tedium—a life always animated by the energy and curiosity, the capacity for humanity and imbroglio, that pervade the Posillipo community no less than all the rest of this extraordinary metropolis.

In the 1860s, when the Bourbon kingdom of Naples evaporated in the unification of Italy, Naples lost the territory, influence, and revenues of south Italy and Sicily. Unlike other dispossessed powers, however, the city itself did not languish or repine. The Neapolitan vitality turned—as E. M. Forster wrote of ever analogous Alexandria—inward: the vigor and ingenuity and, above all, the temperament, formerly exercised in a large realm were concentrated in these few miles of land and sea, known locally as "the Crater." In that unique, civilized, and sometimes explosive liveliness, Posillipo plays its immemorial part.

Today, much of the Posillipo headland is crested by expensive and unlovely new buildings of doubtful legality; and the waterfront road at Mergellina—where, in past years, in the early morning, the fishermen spread and mended their heavy nets—is bedeviled by mad traffic. Continuity, the charm and genius of Italy, has taken some nasty knocks, at Naples as elsewhere. The dread word "development" sounds throughout this fabled coast, from Greek Cuma, just west of Naples, down to the Doric temples of Paestum. Even so, those who live at Posillipo still know their luck and count their blessings—with a nod to our local patron, the nebulous Santo Strata, hard-pressed protector of this ancient hill.

———◄○►———

"Rends-moi le pausilippe et la mer d'Italie"—this was the cry of Gérard de Nerval. Posillipo begins with poetry, at the Roman tumulus long venerated as the tomb of Virgil, in a garden near the Mergellina station. This little hillside park, which contains, also, the austere tomb of the Romantic poet Giacomo Leopardi, who died at Naples in 1837, culminates in the Grotto of Posillipo, the entrance to a road tunneled, in Roman times, through the rock, from Naples to the neighboring Gulf of Pozzuoli. Nearby, the Renaissance poet Jacopo Sannazaro—who in his "Arcadia" presciently dreamed of visiting the vanished cities of Vesuvius—is buried in the red waterfront church of Santa Maria del Parto. In an upper reach of Via Posillipo, Piazza Salvatore di Giacomo, with its congenial restaurant Al Poeta, commemorates the poet whose verses in dialect inspired many of the tender Neapolitan songs. From antiquity, writers, artists, and aesthetes have sought pleasure and inspiration—and solace—at Posillipo. In 1880, Henry James was scandalized by "the fantastic immoralities and esthetics" of an émigré circle here; and declined, for linguistic reasons, to meet another foreign resident, Richard Wagner. In 1897, Oscar Wilde, staying, impecunious and heartsick at Posillipo, completed "The Ballad of Reading Gaol"; while Norman Douglas, living farther out, at Villa Maya, studied marine life along Posillipo in scientific expeditions of a kind recorded, in frescoes by Hans von Marées, in the Naples aquarium. The ghosts of this region are too many—and too vital—to sadden us; rather, they create a company, ironic and benign, to which we ourselves may ultimately hope to belong.

———◄○►———

Like much else at Naples, Posillipo is best explored on foot. The uneven paving of Via Posillipo leads from Mergellina past the enfilade of old villas that, on the left, line the shore. To the right, the nineteenth-century palazzi, with their shops and fruit stalls and cafes and their hung laundry, line the street. On the hillside above, among modern blocks, some countryside can still be seen, and an occasional splendid house, such as the neoclassic Villa d'Angri. But it is the seafront that enchants—even the scruffy stretch of red wall that all but conceals the skeleton of Sir William Hamilton's seaside retreat, the little Villa Emma, where, on hot days in the late eighteenth century, Hamilton escaped the rigors of court and city. Here, from a shaded, elliptical terrace, whose outline is still discernible, Hamilton's celebrated visitors enjoyed the spectacle of the bay and Goethe exclaimed, "There is really no more glorious place in all the world."

The mass, grand and unmistakable, of Palazzo Donn'Anna dominates the rise of Via Posillipo, projecting into the sea like a liner setting forth—or, in certain lights, like a vast, crumbling cheese: in variegation and texture, a colossal Stilton. This great house, whose site is linked to legends of the sirens, has existed much in its present form since the 1640s. A detailed eighteenth-century view, sometimes attributed to Pierre-Jacques Volaire, in the Cooper-Hewitt Museum in New York, shows it in implausibly spruce condition—and devoid of the hardware shop, ice cream parlor, and vegetable stand, and the negligent cats that at present crowd its walls. Evoked for us in the contemporary writings of Raffaele La Capria, Donn'Anna is a microcosm of Posillipo, or of Naples itself: a miniature city of splendor and poverty, passions, pleasures and crimes, conviviality and solitude. Its true precursor is the Roman villa—a shell, but intact—called House of Spirits, along the Posillipo shore at Marechiaro: another cave of Neapolitan memory.

There are palms and pines, then, and sea gardens, and the yellowed hospice for old mariners, all interspersed by tawny villas. The shoreline—for a time obscured by the parklands of large estates—appears again, below orchards and vines. (At a neighbor's table we are given his own excellent red Posillipin wine.) The still beautiful valley of the Gaiola, where an old road leads down to the sea, concludes in the golden rocks and grottoes diversely perceived, over centuries, by countless painters—among them, Hubert Robert and Thomas Jones, Dahl and Ducros, Pitloo, Lusieri and Giacinto Gigante: a scene of ancient fame, as yet unvarnished by the fleeting eye of new tourism.

One needs leisure; one needs imagination. And something more: vulnerability. Vulnerability to time interleaved; to experiences not accessible to our prompt classifications, and to the impenetrable phenomenon of place, which no one, to my knowledge, has ever explained.

IN THE SHADOW
OF VESUVIUS

"THE DELICIOUS SHORES of the Bay of Naples were crowded with villas." So Gibbon describes the Neapolitan scene of two thousand years ago. And the story of this bay is, dramatically, a tale of habitation—of the houses of aesthetes, philosophers, and poets; of the villas of emperors and aristocrats, plutocrats and warriors, and the countless dwellings of their unknown contemporaries: a story formidably evident today and visibly deriving from the ancient world. For no human settlements on earth have exercised a greater fascination than the lost cities of Vesuvius.

Famously destroyed in the summer of AD 79, Herculaneum and Pompeii reemerged in the eighteenth century to change forever, in an infinity of direct and subtle ways, our historic, scientific, and aesthetic concepts, and to extend our always overcautious notion of the possible. The

Great Eruption that shocked first-century Rome reserved its widest—and improbably beneficent—reverberations for the modern era.

Most travelers to Naples will visit those excavated towns on the eastern shore of the bay, less than ten miles from the city's heart, yet in the distinct domain of Vesuvius. They will walk the ancient streets and see the theaters, baths, market, and forum of the cities once consecrated to Hercules and Venus. But most of all they will remember the houses—the Roman houses decorated in inimitable reds, blues and ochers, deep greens, or black and gold, with their astonishing wall paintings and mosaics, their evocation of rites, habits, appetites, opinions, griefs, and pleasures—an intimate way of ancient life laid bare, both poignantly near to us and eerily remote. And all pervaded by a cataclysmic fate. Some visitors will go on to see the more recent excavation of an imperial villa at nearby Oplontis, and the antiquities at Castellammare di Stabia, the ancient Stabiae. Some will ascend the crater for a view, on the one hand, of its enigmatic depths, and on the other, of the incomparable panorama—the bay over which Vesuvius presides not exactly majestically, nor ruggedly, nor with any of the poetic reassurance we seek from Nature, but with the immediacy and infinity of its huge, inscrutable, wanton power. In relation to this, all human encampments must seem huddled, helpless, trivial—and brave. "The mountain," as Charles Dickens noted, "is the genius of the scene."

Observing from Vesuvius the "houses in distant Naples, dwindling . . . down to dice," Dickens was one of innumerable celebrated commentators on the Vesuvian phenomenon; writers, painters, scholars aroused by the reciprocal drama of this prototype volcano and its Roman towns. Through that event of AD 79—an instant, merely, in the immemorial existence of the mountain—Vesuvius broke on human awareness as a supreme destroyer. Yet the Greeks and Romans who, throughout the preceding half-millennium, had sought the rich soil and splendid situation of Vesuvian slopes were not, to their knowledge, thereby inviting disaster. Prior to the Great Eruption, the volcano had been seven centuries inactive, its destructive potential discounted or unknown. Vesuvian wines were celebrated—as is the Lacrima Christi today—and the vineyards shown in a Pompeian fresco were terraced high on the volcanic cone: a cone in that era loftier and more unified than the truncated double peak we now see, reduced by its eruptions to approximately four thousand feet. On that higher cone, Spartacus and his comrades were besieged by Roman troops a century before the Great Eruption. Thick woods gave cover then not only to rebellious gladiators but also to boar and wildfowl, on slopes that in later centuries provided game preserves to successive dynasties of Neapolitan kings.

Sixty years before the Great Eruption, the geographer Strabo noted the mountain's volcanic potential. Sixteen years before the event, a premonitory earthquake prompted not flight but reconstruction. On the afternoon of August 24, AD 79, in the reign of the emperor Titus (whose own visit to Vesuvius is deduced by scholars from an irreverent inscription in a public lavatory at Herculaneum), a man of genius, the elder Pliny—then commanding the Roman fleet at Misenum near Naples—rose from his books to observe a cloud "in the shape of an umbrella pine" ascending from Vesuvius. The events of that terrible afternoon and ensuing night, and of "the dawn that rose like an eclipse," were afterward recorded for the historian Tacitus by the younger Pliny, who described his uncle's doomed attempt to rescue the Vesuvian townsfolk by sea. Pliny the Elder went to his death quoting Virgil—"Fortune favors the brave"; fortunate at least in this: that his story survives and his courage is remembered.

Of the multitude of other contemporary communications doubtless prompted by the Great Eruption, only a handful have come down to us. The epigrammatist Martial mourns the vanished beauty of countryside and towns. And the Neapolitan poet Statius reflects on the future generations who may tread, unknowing, this site of buried cities—a strain taken up in the Renaissance by another Neapolitan poet, the humanist Sannazaro, who in his "Arcadia" recounts a fantastic vision of the buried towns, nearly intact with their towers, houses, theaters, temples—much, in fact, as we see them today.

During the nineteen centuries since the Great Eruption, the Neapolitan experience has been marked by the paroxysms, mild or severe, of a volcano always irresistibly resettled by man. A sixth-century eruption moved the Gothic king Theodoric to absolve Vesuvian householders of their taxes. (Within forty years the Gothic rule of Italy would be extinguished at the foot of Vesuvius by an army from Byzantine Rome led by the eunuch Narses—the battle commemorated yet in the name of a small town on the site: Pozzo dei Goti.)

With the Middle Ages, there began some centuries of quiescence. Vesuvius could never again be regarded as innocent, but the fertility of its slopes—and the human compulsion to play, in this case literally, with fire—drew new communities. Vines again grew high on the cone, thick woods encircled the crater; houses, farms, and villas were built on heights and shore. But in 1631 the volcano broke out in a terrifying episode that took thousands of lives and darkened the sky as far as Sicily. Thereafter, eruptions were intermittent and even frequent until 1944, when the last—or latest—outbreak intensified the agony of a populace living under wartime bombardment and privation.

On that August day of the year AD 79, Vesuvius became an emblem for the precariousness of our life on earth.

Even as the disaster occurred, there were those who saw it as divine judgment—"Sodom and Gomorrah" was scrawled in Greek on a Pompeian wall, presumably by a Jew or early Christian (a detail that would, over eighteen centuries later, interest Marcel Proust). To Neapolitans habitually blending pagan and Christian themes, the volcano also became, through its successive manifestations, a personality against whose rages they implored protection from their patron saint, Januarius. Dark against the sunrise, stern master of lovely surroundings, *Il Vesevo* inspired both apprehension and a curious ironic pride: no mere scenic wonder, but an index of the human condition, a memento mori and a prime source of Neapolitan fatalism. The bay itself, with its encircling hills, is locally known as Il Cratere. Yet never have these people ceased to renew the unequal contest and to build on the volcano.

———◄o►———

Previous concepts of Vesuvius were all subsumed in the eighteenth-century revelation, which began with a crude extraction of ancient sculptures at Herculaneum. Vigorously taken up in the 1730s under royal patronage, and at first jealously concealed from foreign observers, exploration of the ancient towns has persisted through every intervening vicissitude—attracting scholars, scientists, and artists from around the globe, as well as tourists in countless thousands; producing an inundation of works of classical art; galvanizing the sciences of archeology and volcanology and the study of history; influencing our tastes in painting, sculpture, architecture, decoration, and handicrafts. To neoclassicism an impetus, for Romanticism a source. And, above all, a view, inexhaustibly engrossing and moving, of daily life in ancient society.

"Many calamities have befallen this world," said Goethe at the cities of Vesuvius, "but few have conferred such pleasure on posterity."

Vesuvius had become an eruptive force in culture. Depictions of the volcano, surprisingly rare in art before the eighteenth century, now proliferated, as the discoveries attracted a host of Italian and foreign painters—many of them working in gouache, a medium thereafter associated with the melting Neapolitan light and colors. In due course, views of Vesuvius appeared in drawing rooms around the world—and on museum walls, as the greatest artists were allured by the scene and its story, and by the techniques, motifs and colors of the ancient painters. "Colorists like Veronese—a lesson for all my life," wrote Degas, recording in his notebook a passionate litany of Vesuvian tones.

And, from the start, there were houses. In the 1740s, a royal palace was constructed at Portici near Herculaneum, to receive the excavated antiquities that later formed the nucleus of the great National Archeological Museum at Naples. Neapolitan nobility and the well-to-do followed the royal example—as did artisans, engineers, and tradesmen caught up in the Vesuvian boom. Once more, the delicious shores were crowded with villas: the Ville Vesuviane, a testament to Neapolitan heedlessness and inventive grace. Of these new houses, some—by the finest architects of the time—were of airy splendor, with gardens extending to the sea; others stood out grandly on the mountainside; some sought to reproduce the Pompeian form and style; some were confections of the rococo; many incorporated geometrical effects in their matching galleries and double stairs. And each had its prominent image of San Gennaro as apotropea—the exorciser whose powers were being tested to the full.

Erected in a seismic zone, these "case di delizia" with their extravagant ornamentation and facades of colored plaster, their open colonnades and pavilions by the sea, could not long preserve appearances. In 1828, a young Scots visitor to Vesuvius observed that "the houses exhibited an appearance of decay, which was but too emblematic of the people to whom they belonged; yet we were passing through the summer residences of the proud aristocracy of Naples." And Craufurd Ramage went on to censure a lack of architectural "purity" that today delights the eye fatigued by modern uniformity. Now, perhaps, he would think these neoclassical houses another Pompeii, so cruelly have they been used by the elements; by time, wars, and governmental negligence; and by acts of the Vesuvian gods.

Yet this enchanting epoch of Vesuvian houses survives, in perhaps a hundred villas and in innumerable lesser buildings ranged beside them. Many are half-ruined, most are tenements, a few are institutions, others are workshops and garages. Their district begins implausibly on the outlying waterfront of Naples, in the industrial zone of San Giovanni a Teduccio, whose name recalls the emperor Theodosius—

where, in the dusty chaos of Corso San Giovanni, house after house still shows its fine proportions, and the sea is glimpsed through archways that once led down through gardens to the shore. A waterside railway long since brutally divided the houses from their beach pavilions, and the sea itself here is polluted. Yet the long street is lined with a violated and ghostly elegance, which burgeons at Portici as the countryside draws near. There the royal palace dominates over a surge of eighteenth-century buildings and the ruin of the Villa Elboeuf, which, erected in 1711, sheltered the first fruits of the Herculaneum excavation.

At Herculaneum begins the Miglio d'Oro, the golden mile of eighteenth- and early-nineteenth-century villas along what was once the royal road for Calabria. And any traveler to Herculaneum may enter, just past the gateway to the excavations, Vanvitelli's beautiful Villa Campolieto, restored and open to visitors. The adjacent Villa Favorita is still, at this writing, implacably closed. For entry to some of the finest surviving houses—including the royal palace at Portici and the Villa del Cardinale near Torre del Greco— formal permission is required. But at most of the Ville Vesuviane, the visitor who explains his interest will be invited into courtyards and gardens and will often find in the human encounter, as in the houses, pleasure and charm.

The route continues through Torre del Greco to Torre Annunziata—territory, these days, of the Camorra. Or it branches uphill to Barra, and to San Giorgio a Cremano. The villas proliferate, and one has to choose—Villa Faraone with

Doric portico at San Giovanni a Teduccio; Villa Menna and Villa Meola in pastel rococo at Portici; Villa Prota, ornate, phantasmal, beyond Torre del Greco; at Terzigno, the noble simplicity of Villa Bifulco; at Barra, the red remains of Villa Bisignano; or, at San Giorgio a Cremano, the pale, decayed magnificence of Villa Pignatelli di Montecalvo. The stripped yet magisterial facade of this great house, its vaulted atrium, and courtyard where symmetrical stairs are grandly framed by flying buttresses, can be attributed, according to the sovereign authority Roberto Pane, to the genius of one of the most inventive Neapolitan architects, Ferdinando Sanfelice.

Distances are not great, and a local railway from Naples, the Circumvesuviana, serves much of this region. A car is invaluable—and, alas, vulnerable to theft. But the best discoveries must be made on foot, and nothing—except the wayside refreshment—is entirely simple. Yet the journey to the Vesuvian villas is an experience of beauty like a dream: almost illusory, noble, sweet, and touched with tragedy. As ever at Naples, we enter a story so long and diverse, so deeply lived, that even the most clamorous modern change takes on the pathos of the ephemeral; an ambiance that continually sets "The unhappy Present to recite the Past / Like a poetry lesson"—to borrow from another context a phrase of W. H. Auden, once himself a dweller on these shores.

Those who explore Vesuvius should prepare by reading and reflection and should come with a liberal allowance of days. (They should also, for safety, carry nothing snatchable.) The circuit of the mountain by its main road, the old

Via Nazionale, passes through a confusion of millennia, where, among castles and ancient churches, modern "housing" for the moment has the upper hand. Past centuries still make strong signals: a sheep is tethered outside a Laundromat, a donkey or tiny pony draws its cart among the cars. And many a time one sees a man between the shafts, bowed with heat and exertion. To the sanctuary of the Madonna dell'Arco, near Sant'Anastasia, many votaries still make, as in past centuries, their long pilgrimage on foot from Naples each Easter Monday, with altars and banners carried aloft.

Everywhere in these contiguous towns the stalls of Vesuvian fruit and vegetables are conflagrations of color; for countryside is never distant, and any upward detour will quickly end in great stands of umbrella pines and woods of ilex and chestnut. Above, always, is the long rise to the crater or to the older Vesuvian peak called Monte Somma; and underfoot, undoubtedly, the ancient villas lie concealed—suggested, as at Ottaviano, in the royal names of towns.

On the slopes above Torre del Greco, on an outcropping of prehistoric lava, a shaded country road leads to the convent of the Camaldoli della Torre, with a view over the entire bay. On this same sweep of the volcano, among apricot orchards, a shuttered house decays like many of the rest: not large or beautiful, without avenue or garden; distinguished by the fact that here, in the 1830s, a great poet in the last months of his short life contemplated Vesuvius and its ancient towns, and the yellow broom that flowers over the mountain in early summer; and wrote immortally of earth's indifference to our human presence. No one who reads Leopardi's "La Ginestra," from which this house now takes its name, will see Vesuvius without some thought of that great work or visit this neglected place unmoved.

American painters continue to feel the influence of Vesuvius—de Kooning and Warhol among them, and the modern master of Neapolitan light, Randall Morgan. But many New Yorkers—and many other Americans—first glimpsed the Vesuvian drama at the Metropolitan Museum of Art in the reds, blues, and ochers of the Roman room from Boscoreale: an arrangement of one of the finest groups of Vesuvian wall paintings to survive the Great Eruption. These panels in the Second Style—in an architectural perspective recalling the stage settings from which such house decoration derived—were part of a vast treasure excavated in the 1890s near Pompeii, in a district anciently famed for beauty and amenity—the site, once, of a sacred forest and, subsequently, as its modern name indicates, a hunting preserve for kings of Naples. Of the first hoard unearthed there, much was spirited out of Italy and into France in a bizarre transaction involving politicians and bankers and museum authorities. The Metropolitan's room was acquired at auction in Paris in 1903.

Late in 1987, the Metropolitan Museum displayed another set of wall paintings; these were discovered at Boscotrecase, adjoining Boscoreale, at the turn of this century, acquired from the Neapolitan authorities in 1920, and stored since then—apart from one obscure and incomplete appearance—in the Metropolitan's reserve. In the Third Style—of monochrome background with small but predominant painted motifs—these panels carry, on black, red, or white, fine decorations of great interest.

In the 1970s, in one of the strangest episodes in all the history of Vesuvian housing, J. Paul Getty erected at Malibu his representation of a celebrated villa from Vesuvius—a Roman villa, never excavated, from which, through tunnels, classical sculptures were extracted in the eighteenth century, along with hundreds of papyri—the scrolled books of an important library. The tunnels had been closed in 1765 due to leakage of volcanic gas. Now, more than two centuries later, the Villa dei Papiri, with the rest of its ancient library, remains incomprehensibly interred at Herculaneum, while, by the far Pacific, the Getty Museum flourishes in its name.

"Sterminator Vesevo"—so Leopardi characterized the mountain, invoking its ancient name. In the 1980s we build our own volcanoes; and a field of refineries and gas tanks are explosively grouped near the foot of Vesuvius. The great monuments decay or lie with all their knowledge in the earth. Delinquency, official and otherwise, threatens Pompeii itself with a second obliteration. And new apartment blocks rise in thousands, ever higher on the Vesuvian cone, erected by developers who feel little need of appeasing San Gennaro. For the view from these slopes is unsurpassed, and our world is disinclined to draw hard lessons.

"And still," wrote Statius, who had seen the fires of the Great Eruption, "And still the mountain threatens ruin."

CITY OF SECRETS
AND SURPRISES

THOSE WHO LOVE NAPLES are continually challenged to defend the city to visitors who have spent a day or two there, on their way to Sorrento or Positano, Amalfi or Ravello, or to the islands of the Neapolitan gulf. Travelers who have lost wallet and temper in the Naples crush, have been felled by an aberrant clam and bedeviled by chaotic traffic, have stood in that great scene of anarchy and wondered at the city's fame.

They do not take kindly to the devotion Naples inspires in all who know it well. Most galling perhaps is our very acquiescence in the charges: Yes, quite true, the streets are unswept, the museums inconvenient, the services unreliable. Worse still, the twin foundations on which modern tourism rests—restaurants and shopping—are not a prominent feature. Indeed, Naples is often indefensible.

It is also an incomparable civilization in itself, the only city of the classical world, as a Neapolitan writer has said, to survive into our times: "A Pompeii that was never buried." As Venice differs from other Italian cities in having no Rome in its origins, so Naples is distinct for incorporating its Greek past—the northernmost colony of greater Greece in Italy. What remains of that ancient Greece at Naples is not, however, the elevated calm usually invoked as "classical," but rather, the temperament execrated by Juvenal in the Greeks of the first century after Christ:

> Quick of wit and of unbounded impudence, as ready of speech as any orator and more torrential, carrying in themselves any character you please from geometrician to rope-dancer . . . Experts in flattery—and yet believed. If you smile, they split with laughter; if you shed tears, they weep . . . They always have the best of it, at any moment taking their expression from another's face . . . And nothing is sacred to their passions.

Those passions also add much that is somber and tender to the resilient denizens of Il Cratere, as the arena setting of the city is sometimes called in invocation of its presiding genius—the Vesuvius to which thoughts and glances ever turn at Naples, as though to a point of reference, or a sun.

Through a phenomenal continuity of recorded experience here, we know in some measure how Neapolitans have felt in their successive incarnations of nearly three thousand years, dominated by their unpredictable volcano, looking out at their beautiful bay—where, to borrow Byron's phrase, "fame is a spectral resident."

Naples requires time. Goethe, on his first visit, apologized for the absurdity of a mere four weeks' stay. To travelers who offer the insult of a few hours of their time, the city returns its own harsh indifference, plunging them into misadventures and dismissing them. "Covering distance" is meaningless anywhere on the Italian peninsula, where a radius of fifty miles drawn around almost any city can provide delight and interest for a lifetime; it is folly at Naples, where revelations are not instantaneous as at Florence or Rome and need a state of mind that settles on the outsider only gradually, as a revelation in itself. "I tell myself, either you were mad before, or you are mad now," said Goethe under the spell of the Neapolitan siren Parthenope, legendary spirit of the city that grew up around her tomb. "To be enabled to dream like this is worth all difficulties."

What is the mystery into which we are initiated at Naples—this sense of life profoundly informed by awareness of death that values the smallest pleasure as god-given, fatalistically attributing misfortune to the gods' sterner associate, Il Destino? For all its scenic display, Naples is a city of secrets.

If you come to Naples and stay at one of the good hotels on the waterfront, you will enjoy a view of the harbor from windows, which, if you're lucky, look over the Castel dell'Ovo—a medieval construction rising on a fragmentary villa of Lucullus that is open to visitors. The small yacht basin below the castle is busy with private boats in summer and with picturesque traffic all year round. Outside the hotel, however, the surroundings are rather lifeless: pleasant shops are few, litter blows, traffic trundles. The vacant sensation of this quarter of Naples—the once-celebrated zone of Santa Lucia—derives from two relatively recent obliterations: demolition following the catastrophic cholera epidemic of 1884, and the bombardments of 1943–44. In fact, Naples always has something of an air of having survived calamity: it is one theme of her story.

At the top of Via Santa Lucia you will come to the royal palace, on a vast piazza laid out, with magnificent intention, for the Bourbon kings. But the piazza is intersected by traffic, the palace needs repair, the arcades of the basilica opposite are neglected. In the best laid schemes of mice and men, at Naples, the mice tend to win.

————◀◦▶————

Persisting, you will soon discover the opera house, the spacious galleria, and the huge Castel Nuovo that dominates the port. Even so, the city eludes the search for its center. The truth is that there are many centers at Naples, each vital to its own city quarter. And Naples is rifest perhaps at its oldest point, the district of Spaccanapoli, where the city splits along its Greco-Roman decumanus. If (leaving anything snatchable safely behind) you had simply made the brief journey from your hotel to Spaccanapoli, you would have found yourself in Naples indeed.

You arrive in the shadow of the church of Gesù Nuovo and its gem-cut fifteenth-century facade. In mid-piazza, the Baroque runs riot in an ornate *guglia*, the Neapolitan obelisk. Before you lies a labyrinth of Gothic churches, Baroque and eighteenth-century palaces, classical and early Christian fragments, medieval passages and sunlit cloister-gardens. An itinerary can be proposed—if you wish—beginning with the heavenly beauty of the ceramic cloister behind Santa Chiara; continuing to the little Via San Gregorio Armeno, street of the *presepi* makers—craftsmen of the celebrated Neapolitan Christmas crèches—where the church of wildest rococo has a tranquil garden upstairs; and the adjacent Gothic glory of San Lorenzo, where Boccaccio first saw Fiammetta, and where Petrarch spent a rainy night in prayer. Rising on Greek ruins, San Lorenzo also offers a Roman excavation under its adjoining cloister. Nearby, the duomo and its ancient lower church embody the story of Naples. Such suggestions might be endless; but their meaning is inseparable from the area itself, animated with the unquenchable life of numberless shopkeepers, artisans, booksellers, peddlers, and other artists of survival who live along the teeming thoroughfares of Via Benedetto Croce, San Biagio dei Librai, or Via Tribunali.

Here, modern classifications fall away, and we are restored to a world of unregulated, eccentric personality, to
an outlook that encompasses all human possibilities, to faces
and graces—and an intelligence—formed by a longer story
than our own. In this scene of dilapidation and magnificence,
Neapolitans move among their extraordinary architecture
as in a natural element: Even the grandest edifices are not
"monuments" but expressions of temperament in their nobility, their strangeness or sweetness, their theatricality. The
simplicity with which, in all Italy, citizens will treat some
great shrine as a familiar is almost reciprocal at Naples, where
the very buildings draw vitality from the populace, who in
turn seem nourished on color, form, and line.

A New York art critic, exuberantly greeting the arrival in America of an exhibition dealing with eighteenth-
century Naples, tells us that "Naples is poor in mementos
of the Renaissance." While definitions of "mementos" may
vary, there can be few cities, after Florence and Rome, with
grander Renaissance monuments than Naples—the im-
mense gateway of reliefs at the Castel Nuovo, the outpour-
ing of Renaissance sculpture at Sant'Anna del Lombardi,
Giuliano da Maiano's triumphal arch at Porta Capuana,
the stern harmony of Palazzo Penna. Many such examples
come to mind. Yet more often, the Renaissance at Naples
merges, submerges, or reemerges, like all other periods, in
a thousand unannounced details: the mighty entrance of
a crumbling palazzo; a fine frieze or doorway in a scruffy
lane; Pontano's exquisite academy, long a storehouse for

coffins (a development that would not have been lost on the great humanist); or the tomb, by Donatello and Michelozzo, recessed beyond the altar at Sant'Angelo a Nilo. A city of secrets is a city of surprises.

In fact, paradox has as much to do with the outsider's first unease at Naples as with the city's eventual claim on his affection. Time is long here, but a town with a volcano is no place to forget mortality. For a people who see existence as a synthesis, there are no conflicting elements, and Naples offers few neutral zones where tourists can be spared the worst. The puritan view that a sense of pleasure cannot be justified amid visible affliction is meaningless to Neapolitans—who know that pleasure cannot be deferred for ideal circumstances. For connoisseurs of survival, triumph and tragedy are indivisible.

Though modern suburbs offend the sight, the setting of Naples has not changed: from the lovely garden at San Martino, on the city's height, we see the prospect the ancients saw. To the right lies Posillipo—the headland the Greeks called *Pausilypon*, "a pause from care." To the left, where Vesuvius rises, the coast curves past Herculaneum and Pompeii and the recently excavated Opionti. The indentation of Sorrento gives place to an unspoiled countryside of olive groves and villages, on the cape where once a temple of Athena looked across to Capri. And, at the horizon, the outline of Capri itself—its lesser peak, still sacred to Tiberius, and its greater. Even in a land where *bello* is every infant's third articulate word, this beauty is unrivaled.

If the "region of Naples" may be extended, at its southern extreme, beyond Salerno to the Greek temples at Paestum, its northern limit is defined, less than ten miles from
Naples, by the ruins of Greek Cuma—one of the supreme
monuments of the ancient world, little visited on its silent
shore. Between Cuma and Naples lie Cape Misenum, Baia,
and the Phlegrean Fields—the volcanic "Fields of Fire," a
Virgilian landscape of antiquities; and Lake Avernus, entrance to the legendary underworld. For centuries, the now
shabby town of Pozzuoli—known then as Puteoli—held
sway as a foremost port of Europe and a resort of fabled
luxury for the powerful of Rome. Puteoli was the ancient
city, Neapolis the new. Now Pozzuoli looks over its "sea of
marble"—which holds the wreck of a thousand monuments and palaces that lined this coast long ago—to the
volcanic cone of Ischia and the lemon groves of low-lying
Procida.

The modern eye will scarcely focus here. Every promontory and overgrown declivity holds fateful associations;
and the eye of imagination prevails.

From Misenum, in AD 79, the polymath Pliny set out
with quadriremes to rescue the victims of Vesuvius and died
in the attempt. Watching the Great Eruption on that same
August day, his adolescent nephew, the younger Pliny, gath-
ered the impressions he would later record for Tacitus. At
Agrippa's naval yard, still visible beside Avernus, ships were
made ready for the battle of Actium. All around Il Cratere
stand remnants of the lavish villas praised by Statius and

decried by Horace, scenes of leisure, thought, and art—and imperial murders. From this shore, Seneca watched an approaching fleet and identified the Alexandrian mail packets by the trim of their topsails. Here Virgil lived, the poet of this region—who, born a Mantuan, declared: "Parthenope holds me."

"Naples has never been worse," says the pained observer. Really?—not under fascism, or in the degradation and malnutrition of the postwar decade? Certainly, if you come to know Naples you will never cease to rail at its woes—joined in your laments by Neapolitans too courteous, perhaps, to inquire how other societies are likely to look by their third millennium. Glimpses of the arcane, the grotesque, the diabolical will never fail to startle and estrange—compounded, as in most great cities, by modern violence and disaffection. But few days will pass without some fresh discovery of dignity, delicacy, and endurance—when you are not humbled and exalted by acts of human fellowship and inexpressible grace. For myself, each arrival on this shore is a rejoicing. And I wonder at the stroke of fortune that first brought me here to live in intimacy with this civilized spirit and to share its long adventure.

NAPLES REDUX

An Ancient City Arrayed for the G-7

PREPARING IN 1958 to leave his island home in the gulf of Naples, W. H. Auden held that the immemorial allure of south Italy could still impel us to "behave like our fathers and come/Southward into a sunburnt otherwhere/Of vineyards, baroque, *la bella figura* . . ." on a journey of revelation. Even today, when the oxymoronic "refinery"— insanely situated near the foot of Vesuvius—directs its fumes toward the town, or another segment of lovely countryside falls victim to illicit "development," there are those of us who forgive Naples much because of its long private lessons in living and dying.

Such oblique instruction is not for everyone, however. And the modern world of massed material power, which, by mutual and tacit agreement, has bypassed Naples for almost two hundred years now, is in any case less disposed to learn than to tell. It was as if, therefore, by cosmic error, a world event broke loose in 1994 and strayed to Naples. The elected leaders of seven industrialized nations—the United States, Germany, Japan, Russia, Britain, France, and Canada—arrived here for a four-day conference. They were preceded by their respective entourages, constituting some thousands of acolytes, who for a week occupied all the city's hotel rooms, banquet halls, and conference centers, tied up its airport and external roads, and intensified the chaos of its inner traffic. Grand occasions—or their modern semblance—took place in the ornate palaces and ancient castles of Naples, and orations were heard in the medieval rooms surmounting the villa of Lucullus. Lightning visits were made to cultural sites on the periphery—to Pompeii and Herculaneum, to the colossal eighteenth-century Bourbon palace at Caserta, and south to the Doric temples of Paestum—memorials, all of them, to the impermanence of power and the durability of fine construction.

"Security" was invoked to justify all manner of arbitrary disruptions, including the deployment of ten thousand Italian troops and the arrival of an aircraft carrier afloat in the roadstead for President Clinton's protection. The Clintons' hotel suite, on the waterfront, was overlooked from the adjacent rise of the former Greek acropolis by a squad of accredited sharpshooters. Seventy small vessels, fast, serious and gray, and vigilant, were placed around the harbor, seconded by sixty frogmen under water. Fifteen helicopters circled the "aerial space," as the skies were renamed for the event. Nor was subterranean Naples forgotten; the ancient labyrinthine passages and streets that underlie the visible city were patrolled and tested for hidden microphones.

All of which goes to show, as a Neapolitan friend observed, how much our leaders feel themselves beloved.

The event could have offered none of those private encounters, dear to the Neapolitan genius, in which mutual humanity is for an instant established against the odds. The expensive visitors of the G-7 did not arrive, like eighteenth-century milords on the grand tour, curious for important surprises: such visitors bring their importance with them and feel no need of fresh supplies. Their lines of communication were not the meridional graces and glances of the place, but the global filaments of hotline, fax, and cellular phone. For the seven males and their attendant thousands coming south to this feminine township, there would be no rambling into the sunburnt otherwhere. In rooms, offices, and cars, air conditioning insulated them from incandescent July, and from the moral consequences of the notorious south wind, the heavy sirocco that, as Dante noted, carries the sands of Africa into Italy.

One element of the great tradition nevertheless prevailed: the *bella figura*, active on a scale unsurpassed.

Naples, which is a capital of that theatricality intrinsic to the *bella figura*, was once a capital, also, of distinguished tourism. For generations, however, the city has been almost completely bypassed by foreign visitors—a decline that began with the twentieth century and deepened in the fascist era. The *coup de grace* of the terrible bombardments of the

Second World War was, in that regard, compounded by the postwar eclipse of the transatlantic liners to act as a final deterrent. In truth, Naples itself—arcane, disorganized, individualistic—has remained relatively indifferent to modern mass travel and to its imperatives of velocity, sleek restaurants, and "shopping."

Unlike Florence or Venice, Naples long allowed her great monuments to languish in disorder. Her treasures stand, however, in their authentic context—in the narrow animated streets that trace the axis of the Greek and Roman decumanus, in the teeming Quartieri above the port, and in countless outcroppings of decayed magnificence that punctuate the town. Private acts of faith and rescue have not been lacking in recent years—notably from the organization Napoli '99 and its founder Mirella Barracco, whose inspired efforts have brought millions of visitors to the reopened monuments of Naples. With the passage of years, Naples is again becoming a discovery: the last great city of Western Europe with secrets to divulge, existing on her own eccentric terms.

After Naples was chosen as the site for the G-7 conference in 1994, public funds were assigned, under rigorous supervision, for an ambitious program of repair and embellishment of prominent streets and buildings. That decision came from Carlo Azeglio Ciampi, who, as Italy's political structure collapsed under disclosures of corruption, had been called from circles of banking and high finance to be president of the Council of Ministers in the national government. To him, Naples owes a measure of new life.

Throughout the first half of 1994, the city became a workshop deep in dust and discomfort, resounding to a din of work going forward. To many recalling far smaller undertakings that had evaporated in corruption, the present huge project seemed impracticable. Time was short, the Neapolitan character dilatory. The work was not long under way when a new rightist government was elected in Italy, with divisive consequences for public opinion and morale. Above all, the prolonged neglect of Naples had been comprehensive, affecting prosperous zones as well as poor ones, and including unredressed damage from wartime bombardment as well as from the earthquake of 1980.

With astonishment, therefore, one saw a mobilization of practical capacity and public involvement. Innumerable scaffoldings went up and—more improbably—came down to expose the restoration of noble facades and interiors. The handsome but at times near-derelict seafront park called the Villa Comunale emerged pristine from years of vandalism, and squads of blue-clad volunteers set to cleaning its walks and surrounding streets. The royal palace of the Bourbons, and its grand forecourt shared with the church of San Francesco di Paola modeled on the Pantheon, reassumed not only splendor but traffic-free coherence in their relation to each other and to the nearby Galleria and the San Carlo opera house. Coherence, always elusive at Naples, is one effect of the whole renovation.

Urgency gave a stimulus that leisure could never provide, to *fare l'impossibile*. Of the many miles of city streets that
were relaid, a large number were repaved by hand in their
original cobbled patterns by groups of sunburnt workmen
strung out in clouds of dust and acting almost rhythmically
together.

The older streets of Naples are traditionally paved in
large blocks of seemingly indestructible dark lava, or lavatic
stone, fitted like flagstones and pitted, by hand, as protection against their slippery surface. The cobbles, by contrast,
are cut in heavy cubes, between three and six inches square,
and are set in scalloped patterns fixed with asphalt and
sand. These too are usually of volcanic origin, very hard,
and sometimes showing the pinkish cast of porphyry. The
synchronized skill of the work and effect of the interlocking
patterns are fine to see. As with most groups of Neapolitan
workmen, one man will sing—one only at a time, the one
with "the voice"—and the songs are always the traditional
Neapolitan airs, though by no means all familiar.

What could not be accomplished in half a century for
the amenity of the populace was achieved in half a year for
the benefit of inattentive statesmen on a visit. The incen-
tive of the *bella figura* played its part, as did an unpredictable
engagement of public effort and the constancy of an activ-
ist mayor, Antonio Bassolino. Most of the city remained,
of course, unaltered. Our leaders will never experience the
Neapolitan transport "system." They will know nothing of
the older Neapolitan hospitals. (One of these, the Monaldi,

announced the acquisition of a tribe of cats to reduce its rodent population.) What was achieved, however, was not superficial. There was a sustained show of official responsibility—rare around the world these days, and, at Naples, a breathtaking innovation.

PART II *Francis Steegmuller*

THE INCIDENT
AT NAPLES

HONOR AND VIRTUE. Those are the names of two great
crenellated round towers that flank Porta Capuana, in
Naples. This ancient city gate, of the dark southern stone
called *piperno,* was once part of the fortifications of an Ara-
gonese king: a feature of the city walls, where its fellow
towers—still visible at intervals along certain thoroughfares—all bore distinctive names, like Glory and Hope,
Victory and Strength, while still others were known as the
Duchess, the Siren, the Saviour. At Porta Capuana, the decorated white marble arch between the towers was designed
by a Renaissance artist, the Florentine architect and sculp-
tor Giuliano da Maiano. There, just inside the walls, the
Neapolitan law courts are immured in a massive castle—
picturesque, legendary, and grim—set at the rim of the ancient vortex of the city. Outside the gate, a dry moat, then

a busy open ground, site in past centuries of gardens and of a celebrated outdoor theater; now traffic-ridden, populous, poor, and unresolved; exposed, in high summer, to a grimy sun: Piazza San Francesco.

On a Saturday in mid-July of 1983, in the early evening—in broad daylight, as the saying goes—I was knocked down there by two young men on a motorcycle. A familiar story in Italy today: the victim carrying, most indiscreetly, a bag; the assailants—the *scippatori* as they are called in Naples—motorized, swift, skilled at snatching, careless of maiming. The victim, from instinct or defiance, attempts to retain the bag, is in consequence thrown to the ground by the velocity of the motorcycle and dragged some distance—feet or yards—until the bag has conclusively changed hands.

We had been walking, my wife and I, through Spaccanapoli; that is, we had been following the Greek and Roman decumanus that still creates "the split of Naples" at the city's heart. There are two or three of these long, narrow, parallel streets, crowded with grand and decaying monuments, with churches and convents, palaces, arcades: a forest of tiny shops and habitations where magnificence and squalor share a roof. "The great sinful streets of Naples," as an English poet, Arthur Hugh Clough, defined them in the 1840s. Through a hot afternoon we walked, as we had walked a thousand times, along the lava pavements of Via San Biagio dei Librai and Via Tribunali; and, for the first time in years, carried a bag, one of those canvas shopping bags with reinforced handles. We had this unprecedented bag because we had been delivering books for rebinding. At the binder's shop—a slot in the wall of a steep, traffic-flooded alleyway—we had chosen colors of leather and endpapers, exchanged some words with the amiable young man in charge, shaken hands. One book remained in the bag—an old red guide to the city, with our penciled annotations of many years—along with a sweater, a change purse, and a pretty scarf of blue Indian silk. Walking toward Porta Capuana, I held the bag self-consciously folded under my arm, keeping close to the buildings. Without the bag, wearing nothing snatchable, we would have been in no danger whatever.

As we walked, we stopped to enter churches, to look at pictures and altars. Donna Regina was closed, but Santi Apostoli, with its paintings by Lanfranco and its Borromini chapel, was open: these two nearly adjacent churches acutely illustrating the Neapolitan paradox of historic splendor set in poverty. On the tenement beside Donna Regina, a begrimed notice from the Fascist era continued to pronounce those busy dwellings unfit for habitation, while within the church of Santi Apostoli a state of long neglect—contrasting with the restored adjoining monastery—now appeared to border on abandonment (in later years considerable renovation was in fact carried out).

These summer evenings in Naples belong to the poor. By mid-July, the well-to-do have left their modern flats—up on the Vomero hill or along the Posillipo cape—for coastal or countryside villas or for travel abroad. And more modest families are weekending, at least, at nearby holiday "developments" on the Campanian shore. Doctors, dentists, lawyers will be hard to find before September. Many businesses close down, to reopen only at summer's end, and signs announcing long vacations proliferate on shop fronts throughout the town. In the hot mornings, small brown boys trot, barefoot and near-naked, through the town on their way to the sea, and crowds of children appear on the rocks along the harbor front, undeterred by polluted waters or by the consequent prohibition on bathing there—a prohibition seldom observed or enforced. All afternoon, the city languishes in the long siesta, reviving only with the approach of night. At dusk, in the ancient central quarters, shutters are flung back, Neapolitans appear at doors and windows and on the innumerable small balconies that project from upper floors. Men and women and whole families saunter into the cooling streets to take up their parts in the vast theater of city life—a performance in which tourists rarely appear and few outsiders can even claim a walk-on role.

As we passed, that summer evening, through Spaccanapoli, the revival was under way. In a dusty crevice between palazzi, beneath a tiny pergola of grapevines, a family celebration was taking place: a wooden table was crowded with dishes, bowls of fruit, bottles. These people waved to us and called, "But watch out for the bag." In Via Carbonara, where the long, straight street still follows the lines of demolished city walls, the upper church of San Giovanni a Carbonara, one of the supreme monuments of Europe, was closed. Near the foot of its great outer staircase, a woman was roasting American corn on a brazier for a group of barefoot children: "Would you like some? No? Well, goodbye. Watch out for the bag." In the church of Santa Caterina a Formiello, across from the law courts, in the inner shadow of Porta Capuana, a priest called us aside: "This is a dangerous neighborhood. Watch out for the bag." Yes: we were about to take a taxi; we were being careful. "Well, watch out."

——◆◇▶——

Just outside Porta Capuana, we stopped to look back at the arch spanning the roadway between the two towers. Down in the moat, the dry, circular moat, at the foot of either Onore or Virtù—I can never remember which tower is which—a rat was on the prowl. We watched it a few moments as it scuttled in the refuse—a big one, reddish-gray, with yellowed fangs. Then we turned away, to look for a taxi in Piazza San Francesco. My wife—S., henceforth—was the first to spot one: she has a formidable eye for taxis. As she walked into the piazza to hail it, I, too, stepped forward.

The *scippatori* struck instantly. They must have been stalking the bag for some time—everyone we later spoke with thought so—and at that moment, within sight of the taxi, I made things easy for them: I dropped my guard. Unrolling the bag from under my arm, I held it by the handles, down at my side—normally, in fact. I never saw or heard their machine. They came silently, from behind. But when I felt a tug I realized at once what was happening. The well-known and much-rehearsed lesson of what to do at such a moment—*let go*—was forgotten. I tightened my grip. They pulled harder. I held on. I was pulled: pulled down, and dragged. Not very far, five or six yards, my right side bumping along the pavement. I blacked out. I was told later that the motorcycle roared as it sped off, but I didn't hear it. When I came to, a few moments later, there were people around me, talking and trying to lift me from the ground.

For the next few minutes, my understanding is blurred. Memory remains fragmentary. I am carried a short distance and set on a metal chair on the sidewalk. (Later, I learned that the chair had been brought out from a little hardware shop.) Someone is holding a cloth to my nose—a cloth that feels wet against my face. My tongue discovers a broken upper left tooth. Then, suddenly, my wife is on her knees in front of me, asking frantic questions—in English of me, in Italian of those about us. I hear myself reassure her, in an unfamiliar voice, that I'll be "all right in a minute." The cloth is removed from my nose and something cold substituted—small circular ice "cubes" held in someone's hand. They are there only briefly. "*Troppo sangue,*" someone says. "Too much blood." The ice is removed, a new cloth is substituted, which I hold. Now I can see more of what is close to me and directly ahead. From the left, into that field of vision, there comes a hand, holding a pair of glasses—

mine, rescued intact from the street. I take them, murmur thanks, the hand is withdrawn. There is talk around me. I hear "*telefono*" and "*ambulanza*," but a firm masculine voice says, "Quicker to take him ourselves. Come, Signora, we'll drive you." Two pairs of arms lift me to my feet and guide me; then I am being eased into the back seat of a car. S. enters from the other door and holds me. We set off very fast, the driver's hand on the horn.

S. told me later that the driver's companion was holding a white handkerchief out the car window. We had often been spectators of this Italian street drama—*L'emergenza.* Speeding cars bearing ill or injured to the hospital, Klaxon blaring, handkerchief flying, traffic and pedestrians making way. This time, we were the protagonists.

As we lurched in the speeding car, my vision cleared enough for me to become aware of how much blood there was. My second nose cloth was now saturated and dripping, the front of my dark-blue shirt sodden. A rent in the right leg of my trousers showed red gashes and black street grime. There was blood over my wife's white shirt. I was beginning to feel a trickle at the back of my throat, and to wonder what to do about it; I told myself I mustn't stain our rescuers' car. We made a sharp right turn. I caught sight of a large sign: PRONTO SOCCORSO—emergency. We dashed across an open space and stopped. The car door was flung open into a rush of hot air. I heard our driver shout. Then I seem to have passed out again, or become vague: I remember being carried and lowered and hearing S. say, "*Grazie infinite.*" She was thanking my Samaritans; she told me later that they at once drove off, modestly deprecating their intervention.

I am lying on something hard and flat—an insubstantial stretcher, set on the ground. Through its sagging canvas my body touches a cool pavement. Looking up, I see faces staring down at me—the faces of men and women dressed in white. One of the women crouches beside me and begins to wipe my face gently with something soft and cool. She deserves a better response; lying there on my back, I feel my throat filling up and begin to choke; I snatch the cloth from her hand to catch the blood I cough up. As I raise myself to do this, I am aware that something is wrong with my right shoulder. I hear myself ask *"Dove siamo?"*—"Where are we?"—and the answer: "Loreto Mare."

———◄○►———

For a brief time, after we had returned to New York and I was reading here and there in the new red Naples guidebook—the inestimable *guida rossa*—that we had bought to replace the precious annotated copy snatched by the *scippatori,* I tried to find diversion from my battered state by tracing "Loreto Mare"—its formal name, I had learned, is Ospedale di Santa Maria di Loreto—to an ancient, identically named Neapolitan establishment celebrated in musical history. Founded in the sixteenth century, that Santa

Maria di Loreto, where Scarlatti was once a teacher, had been one of the city's "nests of singing birds"—a number of orphanages and shelters for homeless children, whose early students included Cimarosa, Porpora, Paisiello, and Pergolesi, and which formed the nucleus of the Naples Conservatory of Music. But that association of names proved only partly valid. The celebrated predecessor had been destroyed by bombing in the 1940s, and the building to which I was taken, its jerry-built replacement, had inherited only the name, which in common parlance is shortened to a mere "Loreto," with "Mare" added because of its proximity to the Naples waterfront and to distinguish it from a similarly named hospital, Loreto Crispi, in a more prosperous part of the city.

There was, I think, some justification, quite apart from their names, for my confusing this twentieth-century building with one four hundred years older. I had barely glimpsed its exterior walls before my sagging, primitive stretcher and I were placed on a wheeled frame and rolled inside the building; and the ambulance bay itself, as I had seen from my recumbent position, was in a state of dilapidation and decay. (I learned later that the hospital, poorly built in the first place, had suffered earthquake damage in recent years and repairs had been bureaucratically delayed.)

Inside, too, the room into which I was taken was squalid: walls were scarred and marred, equipment was meager. It did not resemble any other hospital I had seen. But the young doctor (his name was Capuano)—bearded in the manner of a Fayum portrait, which he in any case resembled—was deft and humane as, with his equally considerate paramedic assistant, he quickly took up the work the nurse had begun outside: cleaning my face and hands with wet cotton, drying them with threadbare towels, staunching my still-flowing nose with pellets of gauze, peeling off bloody shirt and ruined trousers, gently feeling head and shoulder and leg, treating abrasions, all the time quietly asking questions.

At his direction, I was soon wheeled down a corridor and into *Radiografia*. There, a young x-ray technician, also Fayum-bearded, equally adroit and gentle, apologized for having to twist my shoulder into position for filming. (The twinges left me with little doubt that I had suffered a fracture.) I was helped into my stained and torn clothes and escorted back to the table in the emergency room.

Not that my only companions during the first aid and the filming were members of the hospital staff. S. had been called back to the entry to talk with police, whom the hospital had summoned, but her place was amply taken. Ambulatory patients in white hospital gowns, accompanied by family or other visitors, trooped in from adjoining corridors to learn the news and sympathize with the latest arrival.

"*Ch'è successo? Ch'è successo?*" and, on learning the facts, "*Dio mio! Hai sentito? Da New York!*" Undiscouraged, they followed me into the x-ray room, where they proceeded to watch from behind a partition, pressing sympathy and apologies. "*Madonna! Che orrore!*" or "*Coraggio, Professore!*" Some trooped back with me to the outer room, where we were joined by new recruits and received exclamations of "*Mannaggia!*" and "*Caspita!*" All asked what I had lost in the bag. Several told of friends or relatives ambushed and robbed in corners of the city: "Nobody is safe. What terrible times." I told them that nobody was safe where I came from, either, but they seemed to prefer that Naples enjoy, as it were, a special reputation. "*E veramente vergognoso. Che brutta gente!*" Doctors and nurses came and went as we awaited the results of the filming. No new casualties arrived: it was a quiet moment at Pronto Soccorso.

The two young policemen S. was talking with, she told me later, were courteous. They would, of course, be visiting the scene of the crime, but there was small likelihood that the assailants would ever be identified: *scippatori* usually operated in neighborhoods far from their own; some came from outside the city. As she answered the questions they put to her, her thoughts were elsewhere—on the x-rays that were being taken. She foresaw that these might tell no trivial tale—reveal conditions calling for intervention and perhaps hospitalization—and, unaware of the quality of the care I was being given a few feet away, she saw dilapidated Loreto Mare as a place to depart from. And she thought of our friends Ella and Carlo.

The previous evening, we had dined with Ella and Carlo at a restaurant on the harbor front. We had enjoyed the hiatus of that summer night—the sailboats swaying at their moorings close to our table, the stars adrift in the night sky. How good, our friends had said, to steal a few moments of respite: their house had been undergoing repairs after being damaged in the earthquake; now they were preparing to leave the hot city two days later to attend their son's wedding in Switzerland.

The assumed urgency of finding a new hospital or a private clinic overcame S.'s reluctance to disturb friends seized with their own preoccupations. She concluded her narration and signed the police report. Turning out her buttoned-down pocket of small change, she found one essential telephone token. From a memory not usually retentive of numerals, she extracted their unlisted number.

In the dank earpiece of the hospital's only visible phone, Carlo's voice responded from a more ordered world. "Carlo," said S., "I hate to make this call. I need advice. We are at Loreto Mare." The tale was told in a couple of sentences.

Before she finished speaking, Carlo cut in: "I'm coming at once." Unhesitating human solidarity.

Turning from the telephone to rejoin me, S. found that the two young policemen had followed her, accompanied now by a third officer, middle-aged, with ginger-dyed hair, a thin, foxy face—and yellowed fangs. He was dramatically upbraiding his underlings for having interviewed her before his arrival: he alone, he barked, had the prerogative of demanding details in such a case. They were vainly trying to justify themselves: "*Maresciallo...*" He interrupted them. "Not that it matters," he said loudly, now addressing himself to S. "You must face it, Signora—those thieves will never be caught. Never are. Hundreds of them work this city day and night; they change *quartiere*. But we're not as bad here in that way as you are in New York. You're from New York, I see." He slapped the paper in his hand.

The two younger men showed uneasiness. Chauvinism is unusual, and ill-regarded, in Naples.

S. agreed that something similar, or worse, might have happened in New York.

"Come with me," the *maresciallo* shouted. "I'll take your deposition properly."

But S. refused to go over it all again. "Bureaucracy," she called it. "*Basta con questi discorsi.*"

The *maresciallo* agreed at once. "*Brava, Signora.* Entirely right." And, turning to the others, "You hear what she thinks of your bungling? *Burocrazia, bah!*"

"*They* were perfectly civil." Exchanging glances with the young innocents, S. walked away. She wasn't followed.

———◆———

I am happy to see S. come into the casualty room. She watches awhile, talks with Dr. Capuano, who comes and goes. Somehow, while the work proceeds, we learn a little of the lives of our medical men, and they discover that we are two writers long acquainted with Italy and partly residing near Naples, and that we had planned to leave the city the very next day for Rome en route to New York.

A nurse now extends an invitation to S.: "Would you like to wash your shirt? It will dry quickly in this heat." They disappear together. Time passes.

In the nurses' little common room, S. has cleaned her shirt and put it on again, still damp. From time to time, she goes to the hospital entrance to watch for Carlo's arrival. And now, as she investigates once more, a taxi dashes up the ramp and Carlo jumps out. A brief embrace, wordless, and S. tells him that the excellent care given by Loreto Mare may make a move to a clinic unnecessary. Then Carlo is in the room with me, tall, solid, with a wonderful directness: the practicality that can appear without incongruity in the convolutions of Italian life. He explains that he was delayed by having gone first, in error, to the other Loreto. His handsome presence changes the pace: Dr. Capuano comes in with the x-rays and reads us his findings. (I translate from the hospital file we were later given.)

Cranium: Fracture of nasal pyramid, with opacity of maxillary sinus.

Right shoulder: Fracture and fragmentation of surgical collar of humerus.

Upper lip: Torn.

Upper incisor: Broken.

Multiple contusions on the right side of body.

Curable in ten days. [Which is Italian for "Ten days in the hospital."]

Dr. Capuano says: "The right-shoulder fracture and the bruises on that side are obviously the result of being thrown to the ground and dragged. But the nose and mouth damage can only have come from a direct blow. Since you were unconscious for a moment or two, I'm afraid you were given a knockout punch to make you drop the bag." He goes on to say that the nose needs attention of a kind not available at Loreto Mare, and that he has accordingly telephoned another hospital—Carlo recognizes the name at once—to say that an ambulance will deliver me there shortly. Before I leave Loreto Mare, my shoulder must be strapped, and his assistant will do that work immediately.

The paramedic is a man of early middle age, simple, kind, quietly self-possessed. His own assistant is waiting, spools of bandage in his hands: this is a youth, perhaps twenty, who watches the bandaging from the moment it begins. He is still but eager, ardent, recording every action. There is something impressive about the intensity of his absorption. And, as is so often the case in Naples, he seems, in attitude, in physiognomy and expression, a figure from a seventeenth-century painting, simultaneously impassioned and composed.

The work is done in almost complete silence and with an expertise that makes the manipulation of a broken shoulder almost painless. Almost. When I react to a particular pressure, there is a "*Scusate,*" and, after a few moments, some words about the different kinds of pain resulting from injuries like mine: the break itself, the repair, inevitable weeks of pain and patience. "And then, sometimes, a different pain," the paramedic says. "Not only physical. That, too, goes away eventually." I hear that, and I think I accept it easily, as a warning. Actually, I "forget" it almost immediately. For the bandaging is now completed; the upper arm is strapped to my side; a sling is devised for the forearm. It feels not exactly better but relieved, secure. However, the shoulder begins to ache. Dr. Capuano, consulted, gives me a shot of painkiller—my first since the mugging.

Handshakes all around. S. asks Dr. Capuano about payment. A bill? The Doctor shakes his head. "No bills here. This is a national hospital."

"But we're not nationals."

A smile. "No bills except for special medication, and your husband hasn't had any. Let's hope he won't need any. Good luck!"

Outside, where our rescuers had delivered us, an ambulance has just brought in a new casualty. A young man is groaning as he is carried past us on a stretcher. We are the outbound passengers. Darkness has come on. The night air is hot, thick with gasoline fumes from the nearby shorefront highway. Vesuvius is black above the lighted towns along the gulf. It is 9:30, and we have been at Loreto Mare about three hours.

———◦———

At Loreto Mare, I had noticed that whenever I was on my feet one or another of the attendants was holding my arm.

And now I am not allowed to enter the ambulance on my own, or to sit: I am slid in, prostrate, on the same kind of flimsy stretcher as before. Soon, siren wailing, we are heading for the Rettifilo, the broad, straight avenue that was cut through some of the city's worst slums a century ago as a belated hygienic measure following a calamitous epidemic of cholera. Stretcher and I bounce on the metal floor of the speeding car: my strapping proves its worth, and welcome hilarity accompanies the vain efforts of my companions, reaching down from their seats, to keep me in place. Carlo and S. speak of the excellent care I have been given: if it is equaled in the next hospital, there should be no need of a private clinic. Carlo points out that private doctors are, in any case, almost unprocurable in this season.

What I first see of our destination, as the siren cuts off, is another PRONTO SOCCORSO sign, a short tunnel ending in a vast, dim, silent courtyard, and another pair of orderlies waiting at a door. One small light burns at the entrance of the huge complex of this second hospital. (S. told me afterward that what immediately caught her eye was a sign saying OBITORIO—morgue. Carlo, who saw it, too, was hoping she hadn't noticed it.) In the brief tunnel, a porter's hutch was stained with age-old interior filth. A stretcher is ready, this one on wheels; but, following the shaking up in the ambulance, I prefer to walk. From the dimly lit admissions office—a small, bleak room giving onto the courtyard—we are taken into a tiny elevator. All about us is an older squalor than that of Loreto Mare.

My nose, for a time quiescent, was bleeding again. I began to feel dizzy, confused by a crowd of white-clad figures with strange faces milling about me. Someone eased me into a chair. I heard voices asking S. and Carlo what was wrong with me; and as my head cleared I seemed to be surrounded by a crowd of Pulcinellas—men and women with huge eyes, large noses, and strange mouths. They were inquiring how I felt, and, as at Loreto Mare, expressing indignation against my aggressors. Above the white hospital gowns, the abnormally large eyes were dark-ringed; many faces were bruised, mouths distorted. As I became more alert and responded to their kindness and their curiosity, I learned that these were dental patients, most of them spending a day or two in this national hospital after multiple extractions of teeth—especially wisdom teeth, in some cases all four at once, this kind of surgery being covered in Italy by national health insurance and performed, if one wishes, in a hospital. Again, these people are mostly poor; none would have more than modest means at best. Among them are pretty, sad-faced girls who, perhaps from diseases of the mouth, seem to have lost most, or even all, of their teeth; and elders looking ghostly in their white gowns, like companions of Dante or Virgil at nearby Avernus.

Such was our arrival at the Ospedale Cardinale Ascalesi—"l'Ascalesi," for short—the second of our two Neapolitan public hospitals. This building, we later learned, was indeed ancient, having started life in the fourteenth century as a convent and shelter for "fallen women," dedicated to Santa Maria Egiziaca (St. Mary of Egypt), a penitent fifth-century prostitute. Its transformation into a "modern" hospital had begun during the First World War; in 1931, it had been renamed in honor of a Cardinal in Naples; repeatedly refitted, it had been bombarded in the Second World War and, like Loreto Mare, damaged again by the recent earthquake. To arrive there in darkness and pass under the phantasmal arches of its decaying cloister was to enter in imagination the Hogarthian world of eighteenth-century hospitals—something of the impression one receives, for instance, in London at St. Bartholomew's Hospital, where Hogarth himself has depicted, over the great stairway, the sufferings of the afflicted poor.

But similar, too, to Loreto Mare was the exemplary quality of the personnel. Very soon, there appeared the doctor on night duty—Dr. Riccio, we learned later. Like Dr. Capuano at Loreto Mare, he was young, with a fine face, firm hands. He told us that the *otorino* (so the Italians abbreviate "otolaryngologist"; in America, the short form is "oto") was on weekend call, had been telephoned to at his house on the Vesuvian slopes, and was on his way, a laborious nighttime drive around the Bay of Naples through summer weekend traffic.

Meanwhile, a bed was found, where I should rest before being x-rayed again. (Bureaucracy, Dr. Riccio said with an apologetic smile, required a new set of films.) Two young orderlies appeared and escorted me, one on each side, along the hall. We turned into a good-sized square room with four beds, one of them empty. Unshaded central light glared in a high, fissured ceiling. A scarred plastic wainscot ran around the walls five feet up from the floor; one tried not to imagine the rot behind it. Above, an antediluvian flaking and peeling. On my bed were a clean sheet and a pillow without a case, its ticking stained. My escorts lowered me carefully. Both of them already knew my story. One, stocky and jolly, with a high-pitched voice and a rich Neapolitan accent, volunteered his own *avventura*: in his case, no physical injury but a big money loss. He had gone to a post office and withdrawn his savings to pay for a new car. As he left, a seeming lounger edged him against a building and revealed a pistol in an inside pocket: "Quick—everything you've got." How had he known? His partner, on the watch inside the post office, had adroitly laid a white thread on the shoulder of the chosen victim's jacket. "An old trick, it seems, but a new one to me. The police showed me the thread. Live and learn. We'll be back, *Professore*, to take you for your x-rays." (I am not a professor, but in Naples, where designations are inspired by appearance, one perforce acquires an idea of one's type.)

On one of the three other beds, a lump swathed in a sheet breathed heavily. The two remaining patients were youths. One was playing chess with a visitor, clearly his older brother, perched facing him on the bed. His neighbor had laid out a game of solitaire. Both patients seemed unmarred: perhaps they were to be operated on the next day. After hearing the orderly's tale, they asked me mine, and expressed the usual sympathy and lack of surprise—

"*Purtroppo, Napoli è cosi*"—before resuming their games. Each patient's sheets were different: in Neapolitan public hospitals, family and friends often provide the linen. The hospital expects it. Food as well: the bedside table of each of my three roommates was loaded with wine bottles, bread, fruit, bulging plastic bags, and paper parcels. The air held a homely suggestion of bananas and garlic.

Seeing me installed, S. left to call a taxi. From our hotel she would bring replacements for my ruined clothes and some money and miscellanies; no one yet knew how long I'd be here at the Ascalesi, or where I might next go. (Earlier, uncertain whether S. would be able to leave, Carlo had telephoned Ella to come with a few of his things; we are about the same size.) The two orderlies now returned, and, one on each side as before, with Carlo following, we set out for the new x-rays. Loftiness and solidity—and an occasional segment of vaulted ceiling—were sparse reminders of the hospital's conventual origin; all else was scarred plaster or whitewashed plywood along a warren of featureless corridors. The last stretch of our walk took us through a high, darkened ward of perhaps twenty beds; a single light glimmered at the far end of the center aisle. The room was still. There was a patient in every bed, in most cases recumbent; a few, sitting up in the dark, watched our passage. One or two silently waved. The dim light at the end was at the foot of a flight of stairs. At the top, a nurse led us into Radiology, and for the next half hour my head was filmed again—and again—this time from a greater variety of angles.

During this process, I had seen a youngish man and a very pregnant woman pass through the anteroom and disappear, and it was them—he now in a white coat—whom I found awaiting me when I was taken by my squad to the office of the *otorino.* Giving me his hand and his name— Apuzzo; he was short, dark, and vibrant—he immediately presented me to his wife. "I'm sure you appreciate the reason for my delay," he said apologetically, and they both smiled. "We live on the far side of Vesuvius, and I had to be careful. Weekend driving is dangerous here, as in the States." I wondered a little at his saying "the States" in English, and at his having brought Signora Apuzzo with him for company: she was pretty, and probably slender in her usual state, but her delivery seemed imminent. "It's not often we see an American here," the Doctor said. "We're just back from the States ourselves. We visited New York and Washington. Such beautiful cities! Such splendid hospitals! *Povera Napoli!*" The last words, accompanied by a gesture and an ironic grimace, brought resigned agreement from our companions. "Well, now to work."

Dr. Apuzzo proceeded to give my left nostril what he called a temporary packing, a nurse assisting and the orderlies sometimes lending a hand. He used wet gauzy tape, dyed green by a solution from which he drew it with tongs. His touch was delicate, and he asked several times whether he was hurting; he wasn't, but he pushed firmly, and continued to do so long after I thought the nostril full. I saw that one entire tape had gone in (I couldn't calculate its length); and he began with a second. When he ended, the nostril felt heavily stuffed. A few other attentions ended the session. For a time—perhaps quite a long time, he said—there might be some bleeding into the throat; eventually, it would stop. I should avoid precipitate movement of the head, hold it as upright as possible; the packing should be regarded as an emergency measure, to be removed, for further examination, in a day or two.

He let me look into a mirror: the first glimpse of myself as victim. Not a face but a sphere of contusions. Nose discolored and swollen—in part, certainly, by the bulk of the packing. Across the nostrils and up both sides of the nose, a strip of adhesive to hold in the gauze. Right cheek lacerated and red with Mercurochrome. Pointing to a clot that was beginning to form on my upper lip, Dr. Apuzzo said he had considered stitching the cut but thought it might heal on its own. (It did, and its quarter-inch white scar on the lip's redness is now the last visible trace of the attack.) For the first time, I had a good view of the shoulder strapping done at Loreto Mare: upper arm bound to side, forearm freely resting in its sling. The gap left by the broken-off tooth suggested that I not smile too broadly at my misadventure.

"I'll speak with the *primario*," the Doctor said. "Dr. Riccio. He'll tell you the rest of the story."

I thanked him and his nurse, and asked to be informed when the Apuzzos next visited New York, after the *lieto evento*. He assured me that he, at least, would be coming, eager to visit more of our splendid hospitals. He gave me his card: he

lived, and had his private practice, in a small town called Pog-
giomarino. "Despite its name, it's not on the sea." Now, after
the careful drive to the city, and the painstaking work—he
had been with me over an hour—they would drive carefully
home. The baby would be born in the country. "We love the
country," he said. "You must visit us." Handshakes; and the
four of us walked back, as we had come, through the darkened ward and the dim, dingy halls.

Outside "my" room we find a party in progress. Ella has
arrived, and she and S. are in the corridor: their lovely faces,
their contrasting beauties—dark and fair—and their pretty
clothes (Ella an angel in blue and white linen, S. a Modigli-
ani), their air of summer health and well-being. And, chat-
ting with them, even at this hour, a dozen or more patients.
Though I now see them clearly, it isn't only my vision of
them that has changed. Most of the women patients, and
some men, have shed their hospital gowns and are in pajamas, plain or fancy; one or two of the women are wearing
print wrappers. The arrival of the foreign visitors has lifted
spirits, created a diversion. The faces with the darkly circled
eyes and marred mouths are more animated now. Everyone greets me. How do I feel? Better? I already look better!
All will be well, *Professore*; everything passes away. Such is
life; such is fate, our destiny.

It is well after midnight. The orderlies insist on help-
ing me back onto my bed. But I no longer feel the need or
the wish to be there. The firmness of Dr. Apuzzo's packing

has given confidence: alertness returns. I wonder how long I have been away from the room. An hour? Two hours? The chess game is over; the brothers are talking in low voices. Beside them, the solitaire, too, is completed; the young man lies on his back, staring at the ceiling, where the yellow bulb still burns.

I pazienti. And I am thinking of the Italian word *patire,* which means "to suffer," and feeling that these fellow patients of mine embody, in their very definition, pain, endurance, and a certain needful philosophy.

There is a change in the third bed: my arrival has been heard. From the sheet emerge first the head, on two pillows, then the pajama-clad body of an elderly man, several days unshaven. He sits up, rubs his eyes and his white-stubbled jowl, stares at me and my bandages—and, seeing me sitting up against a single pillow, at once silently offers me one of his. The corridor sounds are subsiding; out there the light had dimmed. And suddenly I sense a greater silence as well—beyond the open window. A hush has descended: yes, even over Naples.

———◄○►———

As I look back now, I realize that all those details following my return from the *otorino,* still vivid to me today, were compressed within a few moments—that, in fact, scarcely was I on my bed when S. and Ella and Carlo were with me, and I was changing into a pair of Carlo's white cotton pajamas, brought by Ella. The jacket, as it brushes against my lip, at once shows a spot of red. We talk in low voices, the three perching around my bed. We speak of the patients in the hall, of human kindness and medical skill. Ella tells of a road accident in Holland when she was thirteen. It was at the end of the war. She had suffered privation, malnutrition. The accident brought face injuries, plastic surgery in Sweden, her mother's country (we had always noticed a faint scar)—the surgery, with local anesthetic, so painful that she begged her mother to stop the doctors. Now she is grateful to have gone through with it. Looking about my hospital room, she says, "To think that last evening we were sitting by the sea, serene." And I hear S., seated on my bed, quote Petrarch on the unpredictability of existence:

> *O nostra vita, ch'è sì bella in vista,*
> *com' perde agevolmente in un mattino*
> *quel che 'n molt'anni a gran pena s'acquista.*

That sense of human helplessness under the vicissitudes of existence is now to become more acute for me always: an indelible remembrance of Porta Capuana.

 We are quiet, even tranquil. This unlikely being together, the four of us, here, in the earliest morning, amid the suffering of others: these uncanny few moments of peace.

———◀○▶———

Dr. Riccio, appearing at the door, asks S. to accompany him; and she, soon reappearing, beckons to Ella and Carlo. Ten minutes or so pass, during which I'm again required to recite my mishap, this time to the old man who has offered me his pillow. He expresses an unprintable opinion of my assailants. Reenter Dr. Riccio with my wife, both smiling. The doctor addresses me. He has had messages from Dr. Apuzzo. First, the x-rays suggest no grave head damage. (Dr. Riccio interjects, "You can thank God for your luck. Such muggings can be fatal.") Second message, a repetition of what I had already been told: in three days, removal of packing, and reexamination. I am welcome—more than welcome—to stay at the Ascalesi until reexamination, says Dr. Riccio. In fact, he would officially advise that I do so. But he knows—my wife has pointed out—that in less than three days we can be at home, where we now must dearly want to be, and where our own doctors can take over. Dr. Apuzzo having expressed no objection, Dr. Riccio can, on one condition, release me: we must sign a document assuming responsibility for leaving the hospital.

For a pair of New Yorkers, there appears to be no choice. Nevertheless, S. carefully reads the necessary paper and signs it with hesitation: it states that I am leaving the hospital *contro parere sanitario*—against professional opinion. Carlo goes to telephone for a car to take us to our hotel. Soon, over his borrowed white pajamas I am slipping a long raincoat—another of Ella's provisions. S. gathers together our few belongings.

Once again, there is no question of payment. We are not even permitted to make a donation.

Dr. Riccio has his way of seeing us off. "Your shoulder—isn't it acting up again by now?"

"A little."

"Just a moment."

A quick injection, handshakes all around, and the four of us are in the tiny elevator.

Carlo has telephoned one of the Casillo brothers, a pair of genial drivers who act as freelance chauffeurs for a number of Neapolitan families—and, by extension, occasionally for us. We had, in fact, engaged a Casillo—we never know which one will turn up—to drive us to Rome later that day. And now one of them, roused from his bed, is awaiting us beside his car in the huge, dark, vacant hospital courtyard. As we emerge and walk toward him, his eyes enlarge. In retrospect, his shock and words of sympathy merge in my memory with those of the night porter at our hotel, where Casillo delivers us a few minutes later, after a swift trip through a ghostly city—a city free, at that hour, of the strangulation of traffic. The phantom in Dr. Apuzzo's mirror had been no great surprise to me; my fellow patients in the hospital were accustomed to disfigurements more drastic than mine; and Carlo and Ella, who would doubtless have muted their dismay in any case, had both been forewarned. But the shocked reactions of our driver and of the hotel's night concierge now bring home to me how startling I must appear to others in my new "public image."

Carlo's parting words, as we embrace at the hotel doorway: "Be sure to get the morning paper. You may be in it."

Wrought up and exhausted, we go to our cool, beautiful room. The curtains have been drawn against the dawn. The sheets have been turned down, our slippers placed on bedside mats. The beds are soft, luxurious, and inexpressibly welcome: a return to good luck. Yet the consciousness of the suffering and squalor and of the skill and kindness we have just come from is intensely with us as we turn out our lights for a few hours' sleep.

We have had a bad experience, even a hideous one. Having survived it, however, we have the means and ability to extricate ourselves from its most sordid realities and to lick our wounds in privileged conditions. We have checkbooks, credit cards, passports. In my briefcase, on a desk near the windows, there are two plane tickets for the following day. We are experienced in organizing departures, adept at the science of travel. Since my injuries are not incapacitating, we have been able to take up our few belongings and leave the Ospedale Ascalesi and its patients to their unchanging fate. The unfairness of this contrast is not lost on us. From a

generosity that is profoundly Italian, and particularly Neapolitan, no one has made us feel it.

We wake, of course, to the onslaught of our new circumstances. S. is up quickly, to dress and do our packing,
and to go out to make an official report of the crime at the
Naples Questura—the police headquarters. The Questura
will provide her with a confirming document that we will
need in New York—not least in connection with insurance
claims for the prospective American medical expenses, already mounting in the mind's eye.

It is a burning, brilliant morning. I lie in bed looking at
the volcano, wonderfully clear in the dry air, and at the sails
of innumerable small boats setting out for Sunday regat-
tas. An hour passes, perhaps two, and S. returns to tell me
of her expedition to the Questura, in via Medina: a walk of
fifteen minutes through hot, depopulated streets, past the
decrepit palaces of Pompeian red and the great dark castle
of the Angevin kings—the castle known in Naples as the
Maschio Angioino, in accordance with the south Italian tradition that a show of power is ever masculine.

Two uniformed police, each with *il mitra*—that is, a machine gun—were on guard at the entrance to the Questura.
After explaining her mission, S. was directed into a featureless ground-floor office, where her *denunzia* would be made.
She seated herself at a desk where a slight young man in civil-
ian clothes was sifting a stack of papers. When, putting his papers aside, he quietly asked her business, his mild, considerate
manner was disarming in the grim setting. And as he copied

her information on a long, lined form, their questions and answers became a discussion rather than an interrogation. In return for her name, he politely offered his own—Giovanni Cannavacciuolo—and they exchanged a smile for the shared difficulty of unwieldy names. Having inscribed her profession, of writer, he laid down his pen to ask earnestly, "And what future, Signora, do you see for the arts in such an epoch as our own?"—a question that occupied them for some time. Giovanni Cannavacciuolo went on to speak of his tiny property, no more than a field, in the hills south of Naples, which he would probably never have the means to build on, but which he visited whenever possible, merely to sit in silence looking out over countryside and sea. Friends and family urged, at times, a more practical outlook. He appreciated their reasoning, but doubted he would ever cut a wide swath in the contemporary world. Ironic but not unhappy smile.

Their transaction completed, these two stood up and shook hands. "How do you propose to return to your hotel?"

S. said she would walk.

"No. I'll telephone for a taxi—if only because, after such an experience as yours, my dear Signora, one may feel too solitary. Let us spare you at least that lonely walk." In via Medina, he handed her into the waiting cab.

———◄○►———

S. has brought back with her the morning paper, the Naples *Mattino,* but we do not figure in the crimes of passion and dispassion reported there. I think how easily I might have been summarized in two lines: a defunct, incautious tourist.

At noon, half a dozen members of the hotel's staff assemble at the main door to bid us a quiet and solemn farewell. They perhaps believe that, having welcomed us on our Neapolitan arrivals over so many years, they are now witnessing our last departure. I am then carefully settled in the car and do my best to hold my head in the advised position as Casillo drives us north through the lush midsummer of Campania and Lazio.

——◄○►——

The hotel in Rome, where we had reserved "our usual" room, was already aware of my mishap. In telephoning that morning from Naples, S. had asked that a doctor call on us late in the afternoon. Now, following another kind welcome, we established ourselves in the familiar Roman room, I have something like a bath, we are alerted of the doctor's arrival by a telephone call from the hall porter, who accompanies him upstairs and introduces him.

An elegant young man—though no more so, in his well-tailored street clothes, than his Neapolitan counterparts in their gowns—Dr. F. tells us he has just come from duty at one of Rome's largest hospitals where he is in the department of internal medicine. He has been sent to us, at the hotel's request, by the International Medical Center, which maintains a register of doctors speaking foreign languages. After hearing our story—not in a foreign language—he checks my bandages, glances into my throat, asks how I feel, and, on a sheet of his stationery, rapidly writes, "No objection to travel by air," together with my name and his own; and on another sheet he jots three prescriptions—one for *cotone emostatico* (blood-clotting cotton, in case my nose injury should hemorrhage on the plane), one for painkilling pills (he has himself given me a preliminary shot), and the third for an antihistamine. His fee for these services—he is a very efficient young man, and has been with us for fifteen minutes all told—is a hundred thousand lire, at that moment, the equivalent of seventy dollars. S., having divined the sum, has the money discreetly ready in her hand. It is no more, perhaps much less, than a doctor in a great American city would charge for a similar Sunday house call. My Neapolitan doctors, who provided hours of free care in their hospitals, might conceivably ask the same if they were called in privately—since they, I have learned, maintain private practices. Dr. F.'s services in the Rome hospital to which he is attached would, in turn, be free.

S. had made two other telephone calls that morning: one to the answering service of our New York physician, describing my injury and asking for an emergency appointment on our arrival in New York next day; and the other to a Roman friend, who now arrives at our hotel room door. This is Giulio C., a political analyst on the staff of Radiotelevisione Italiana. He has driven in from his beach house at Fregene, west of Rome, where we were to have dined that evening. Sunburned, vigorous, in jeans and white shirt, Giulio sits by my bedside, commiserates, and, as though in deprecation of his radiant appearance, cheerfully recounts an experience in the mountains of Greece, where, one summer, he was riding pillion on a friend's motorcycle. Striking loose gravel on a sharp curve, both men were thrown to the ground and badly scraped. The nearest village being without a doctor, emergency treatment was provided by the proprietor of the local café, who without prior warning poured methylated spirits on the travelers' wounds. "Everybody enjoyed our screams," Giulio recalls. "Especially those of my friend. He's a tenor, and gave them high notes from arias until the agony abated." Nostalgic pause. "They loved it. A musical people."

We laugh, we talk a while, and once again feel comforted. As Giulio ends his visit, he assures us that we will have an easy flight, next day, with Alitalia—words we take to be simply an expression of his optimism.

At Rome airport the next morning, however, we find that Giulio has been active. When we ask to exchange our economy reservations for first class, we learn that he has been in touch with a tenderhearted friend in the airline offices; and we are now offered, with the compliments of the company, "in consideration of the incident at Naples and of your long loyalty to Alitalia," a pair of front seats in business class—as spacious as anything available "upstairs," and more secluded. We install ourselves, and throughout the flight I am cosseted with hot and cold towels, extra helpings of dessert, and good-humored sympathy from the chief stewardess, whose name is Nadia. Dr. F.'s painkiller is effective; the packing holds firm; bleeding into the throat is not excessive. And I doze off.

At Kennedy, Alitalia has a wheelchair waiting. Our baggage appears quickly. Customs waves us through. The taxi-driver is indifferent. Home at last.

———◁○▷———

Were we spoiled, perhaps, by the immediacy of care and human fellowship shown us at Naples? Unreasonable in expecting something of the same concern in New York? Now, established in our apartment, we discovered that my predicament had somehow run out of urgency en route, that senior medical specialists in New York are no less inclined than their Neapolitan counterparts to desert the field in the summer months, and that the status of outpatient at one of the city's greatest hospitals can involve interminable waiting, demoralizing anonymity, and a sense of removal from the normal reciprocity of existence. Yes: outpatient. Having signed myself out of one hospital against professional opinion, I was now assigned, at another, the status of outpatient—which, it was felt, would assure me more serious attention.

By no means subscribing to the hypothesis that order drives out compassion, I yet could not help contrasting—on the day following our return to New York—the air of haste and condescension diffused by my new *otorino* with the simple kindness shown by his recent predecessor. In the shabby Ascalesi, Dr. Apuzzo had wistfully recalled just such splendors—of pastel carpets, polished desks, and gleaming walls—as adorned this new specialist's suite of rooms within the hospital, where the great man and his staff of assistants, secretaries, and receptionist pursued their tasks, and where long windows gave on to summer lawns and the river.

Having extracted, with pincers, Dr. Apuzzo's long tape from my nose, this doctor cursorily inspected my nostril before handing me over to his assistant, a pleasant young woman, who arranged for yet another battery of x-rays. That evening at home, a neglected remainder of the packed tape began working its own way from my nose. I was able to extract the entire second length of it (the first inserted, and therefore the bloodiest), and the next day, to set at rest the apprehensions of the x-ray technicians, who had meanwhile reported its inscrutable presence. My new oto himself wasted no time in regrets for his oversight: "That Italian certainly did a hell of a packing job."

Another onslaught of x-rays was now required.

I mentioned increased bleeding into my throat.

"Just plug that up." S. has already done so, using the cotton prescribed in Rome by Dr. F. "Shouldn't give you trouble."

That night, I awaken to find blood pouring from my nose. We hastily dress and take a taxi to the hospital's emergency room, all the while attempting to staunch the flow—and unhappily reminded of our precipitate journey one week earlier to Loreto Mare.

It is after midnight. It is, in fact, the early morning of July 23, and I am speaking of the year 1983. Entering the hospital, we find ourselves in a curious atmosphere. Some hours earlier, the singer Diana Ross had given a free concert on the Great Lawn in Central Park. After the performance, gangs of thugs ambushed, attacked, and robbed segments of the dispersing audience and others in the vicinity; and any number of shocked and beaten victims had been carried to hospitals for emergency treatment. Making, in the wake of these events, our own bloodstained appearance on this hospital scene, we represent, perhaps, a last straw for that night's exhausted and distracted staff. In any case, we have a desolate wait—much of which we spend coping with forms and mopping my face, sometimes simultaneously. The few other chairs are unoccupied. A television set flickers over-head, mercifully inaudible. It is during this long interlude that my eyes, above the dripping towel, meet my wife's and I say, "Let's go back to the Ascalesi."

Two hours and a large ice pack later, we are again in a taxi, on our way home. It is perhaps 3 AM, and we are becoming reluctant experts on predawn conditions in the world's great cities. We are also learning something about urban violence around the world.

Informed about the bleeding the following day, my cheerful specialist discounts the likelihood of recurrence: "A little blood looks like a lot."

Two nights later, in the course of a violent and frightening hemorrhage, we return to the emergency room; and, after another dismaying and dehumanizing wait, I receive my first serious examination since reaching New York. My oto (and I have already decided to relinquish my claim on him) has on this occasion alerted his young resident at the hospital, and she—proficient, pretty, and kind—takes me in hand, gives me meticulous attention, and admits me to the hospital. There I remain for a week, recovering not only from my wounds but from the exhaustion and discouragement of recent days and reflecting, in my bright, expensive room, on diverse aspects of what is now apparently called "caring" and used to be called "humanity."

I reflected, not least, on that very question of language: of mighty words displaced by flimsy ones; of sentiment turned to sentimentality, and essentials debased into pleonastic "situations." Even the kindest of my new hospital attendants—and many were very kind indeed—spoke to me across an artificial barrier of polysyllabic indirection, where my "stressful situation" was being "checked out," and where I could never simply be told but must everlastingly be "notified" of my "ongoing status." All my Neapolitan rescuers had used direct, expressive words, words still vigorously derived from human experience: none had lost—as yet—the power of valid speech, or been persuaded to embrace pretension in the name of professionalism. And I wondered how long their luck might hold.

I also pondered what Gibbon might have called the rise of brigandage around the world. I wondered about brutality: its many faces—some of them official ones—and its consequences, both personal and global. And if I thought about affection and friendship, and about civilization itself, these appeared more precious and more precarious than before.

My hospital days passed. I became an outpatient again, closely familiar with the waiting rooms and stacked magazines of oto, orthopedist, and other healers. At the call of my name—of my first name only, as it often was—I would enter the doctor's bright office, carrying my ever-replenished set of x-rays. My head and shoulder gradually ceased to pain me; and my ear ceased, also, to miss the note—not only of concern but of the personal—for which it had been so grateful in Naples. If there was a question to be asked, one learned to have it ready and to speak quickly, for one's moments with these specialists were few. One doctor in particular was like an indifferent priest opening and closing the slide of his confessional on a busy Saturday night. Medical friends tell me that, among New York hospitals, Bellevue holds something of the place of the Ascalesi and Loreto

Mare, and that I would have found there something of the same devotion.

———◄○►———

Throughout these weeks, I had occasionally remembered the warning given me by the paramedic at Loreto Mare who devised my first sling. That evening in Naples, as the young assistant watched with his rapt and tender attention, the older man had spoken of the "different pain"—of the mental anguish that can follow such a brush with one's fellow beings, such a loss of control over one's existence. When, from time to time, I recalled his words, it had been to congratulate myself on my sustained good spirits—continually remarked on by friends—which seemed to have withstood both the experience itself and the rough-and-tumble of my New York medical adventures.

Depression did come, however. It appeared abruptly, when my final Velcro sling had been discarded, my breathing was clear, my lacerations had healed; when my teeth had been ingeniously repaired; when the first of the formidable bills had arrived and been paid. But that "different pain" into which I was morosely plunged took its changing forms through several somber weeks. Like Joseph Conrad's victim of another Neapolitan mugging—in his story "Il Conde"—I was "shocked at being the selected victim, not of robbery so much as of contempt." From all this, too, I eventually surfaced—thanks to affection, to friendship and professional skill, and to time itself.

———◄○►———

About ten weeks after my "incident," we returned to the Gulf of Naples. That season, when the grapes are being harvested all through Italy, is perhaps the most radiant of the year. We have often spent it on Neapolitan shores, and one brilliant morning of this particular October, we paid a series of visits in the city itself.

As we drove up the ramp at Loreto Mare, I saw that a patch of worn turf, scattered with refuse and planted with a pair of stumpy palm trees and a clump of dusty oleanders, preceded the entrance to PRONTO SOCCORSO—that paved entrance where I had lain on my first stretcher. A few yards away, the cars, trucks, and trams roared and rattled on the waterfront road, past the church of Santa Maria del Carmine and the unrepaired effects of the bombardments of 1943. The young Dr. Capuano, Fayum-bearded, was again on duty. Shaking hands, he approved my appearance with a quiet smile. We talked a little in the shabby room where I had received such fine attention, and where I now felt more poignantly than ever the odds stacked against this valiant staff. Taking us to the rear of the hospital, Capuano showed us a small group of masons and plasterers at work on a ruined corridor—municipal workers at last assigned to tackle the earthquake damage of 1980. We left our thanks for the considerate radiologist, and for the philosophical master bandager, whose warning I had first undervalued and later understood.

Next, the Ascalesi. As our taxi entered the covered passage leading to this second hospital, S. showed me the "OBITORIO" sign—cryptic in all senses—that had done little to relieve her spirits on our earlier visit. The ghostly predawn quadrangle of ten weeks before was now in full sunshine and crowded with cars, ambulances, and busy Neapolitans, the meridional nature of the scene once more emphasized by a group of palm trees. I could now see that the courtyard was lined on three sides by lofty arcades—the arches shabby and decayed but noble still. Fitted between the arches, a barbershop and a tiny bar; in the latter, a group of white-clad clients clustered at the espresso machine.

On the taxi ride from Loreto Mare, our driver, whose forehead was bandaged, had expressed approval on learning our destination. During the previous night, he had suffered a head injury; and would be glad to have, at the Ascalesi, an injection for pain that was beginning to trouble him. By way of explanation, he added that he was Puteolan—a native of Pozzuoli, the ancient seaport that is now a western suburb of Naples. His explanation was, in fact, clear to us. For many months, Pozzuoli had been experiencing an acute new series of its immemorial seismic shocks: the phenomena of bradyseism, which causes land to rise or fall. Each day, at Pozzuoli, houses were crumbling and inhabitants being evacuated. "It was our turn last night," our driver told us. He had seen his wife and children safely installed with relatives in Naples, and had set out to work as usual. But the trauma was beginning to make itself felt, and he would ask for a little attention at the Ascalesi.

As we entered the hospital, we immediately discovered the cheerful orderly who had recounted the theft of his savings. With a roar of "*Dio Mio!*" he opened his arms and gave me, to my astonishment but not displeasure, a delighted hug. A new wave of bandaged patients and their visitors drew round to hear our history, and to show—like all good listeners to a tale—first horror, then suspense, then relief and joy. Tears were shed for this return of ours, this act, as it was called, of faith and solidarity.

Now the father of a healthy daughter—"*una bella femminuccia*"—Dr. Apuzzo greeted us warmly. Drawing us into his little office, he carefully examined my nose and congratulated me on the exemplary treatment administered by those wonderful New York hospitals he longed to revisit. He waved away my thanks for his own skill—no novelty, as he supposed, to one familiar with the expertise of the New World.

As we emerged into the Ascalesi courtyard, we saw that our driver's bandage had been changed. He now felt, he assured us, quite equal to taking us on our last call. So we found ourselves, on that beautiful autumn day, back at the massive towers of Porta Capuana: Honor and Virtue. We looked up, as before, at the sculptured arch of Giuliano da Maiano, and down at the moat where, the previous July, we had watched the scavenging rat. We walked across the strip of road where the *scippatori* had struck and I had injudiciously kept hold of our bag.

On that July day of the "incident," a chair had been brought out for me. My glasses had been retrieved, and ice held on my wounds. And we hoped now to leave our thanks for these and other gestures that, in their way, had contributed much to my recovery.

As you emerge from Porta Capuana, there is a café on a nearby corner, almost facing you across the roadway—the roadway where, long ago, there were gardens, and where, in seventeenth-century summers, the players acted in their open theater. At the café, we now introduced ourselves and made our explanations to a youngish man standing by the cash desk—a man who, dressed in sports clothes rather than white jacket, was clearly in charge, perhaps the owner. He showed no surprise. It is a neighborhood, after all—or an open-air theater—that has presumably seen everything. But he heard us with close attention and, after a short silence, said he would relay our thanks to those concerned.

He then said, after another pause, "I remember that afternoon very well."

Our turn for silence.

"I had the child in my arms." He was looking at us in the same way as before, unblinking. "I had just lifted her from the stroller. Then the *scippatori* arrived. Fast." Short pause. "Making their getaway, they knocked over the stroller. I'd taken her out of it the moment before they crushed it."

The three of us stood there without a word.

He said, "She's all right." Then, "You look all right, too."

I agreed that I was.

"That's good," he said. "Well . . . And now, what will you drink?"

CODA   *Shirley Hazzard*

PONDERING ITALY

SINGLY OR IN BATTALIONS, the travelers still descend on Italy in expectation of happiness—a hope at odds with our skeptical world, and yet, in that place, often requited. Few experiences compare in reliable enchantment with the transalpine or transoceanic arrival on the inexhaustible peninsula—an entry that suggests a reunion, an achievement. (In the momentous year 1776, Samuel Johnson, perversely turning his attention to the Old World, observed that anyone "who has not been in Italy is always conscious of an inferiority." We might add that those who have managed it are usually aware of their good luck.)

Like luck itself, Italy cannot be explained. We arrive, from modern cities and societies that have all the answers, armored with explanations. If we have any sense, we will for a time fall—not silent, but into a state of receptivity; for Italy, which harbors mysteries and arouses imagination, does not supply solutions. A sense of relief felt by visitors

springs, rather, from being restored to unclassifiable experience: we are encouraged to stop defining life, and to live
it. The element of chance regains importance; we recover
the capacity for astonishment, and the gift of taking some
things for granted.

Those of us who first came to Italy in the 1950s were
more than lucky: we were blessed. The timing was itself
a stroke of destiny, in the aftermath of the receding war,
and in the moment of hope. We were surprised by pleasure,
which had never been quite acceptable in our own coun-
tries; and which came, in Italy, with simplicity and inexpressible charm. One was young, and needed little in the
way of material trappings. The day was an adventure of discoveries, mortal and immortal, inward or external, and occasionally somber. There was loneliness, loveliness, grace,
grief, a prevalent civility, and, when misfortune struck, a
prompt humanity. The impressions that poured over us in
those years and our own readiness to be pleased can never
be mocked or repudiated. One was learning to look, to re-
spond, to value the moment and the gesture; coming to
know—and, once in a while, to forget about—oneself. One
was the object of a lively, and ancient, curiosity. And the
word "Beauty," ever on one's lips, never staled.

It was not an affluent era. All Italy had been a battlefield.
In cities, there was frayed grandeur, shabbiness, need, with,
here and there, tints and textures of an exhausted splendor
that cannot recur. Nothing was pristine, except the light.

In the Italian way, one always got more than one asked for. There were heights and depths, shocks, disappointments. The tumble into the viscous canal could never be bracing in the manner of cold crystalline waters; but gave its own invigoration.

There have been, since then, successive Italies and successive selves. Today, as in the past, Italy is often indefensible—if no more so, perhaps, than nations that proclaim their virtue. What lingers are those saving graces that have drawn the centuried gratitude of travelers, and—beyond all emblems of the new "success"—some unfailing human engagement with the unfolding of existence.

PHOTO CREDITS

Page ii: David Alan Harvey, *Naples, 1998.* "In the morning, fishermen prepare their nets and set sail." © David Alan Harvey / Magnum Photos (NYC15986).

Page viii: Herbert List, *Palazzo del Duca di Marigliano, 1960.* © Herbert List / Magnum Photos (PARI84693).

Page 8: Henri Cartier-Bresson, *Naples, 1960.* © Henri Cartier-Bresson / Magnum Photos (PARI8892).

Page 10: Henri Cartier-Bresson, *Ischia, 1952.* © Henri Cartier-Bresson / Magnum Photos (PAR57810).

Page 68: Bruno Barbey, *Naples, 1964.* © Bruno Barbey / Magnum Photos (BABII07).

Page 70: Herbert List, *Galleria Umberto I, 1960.* "A covered shopping arcade." © Herbert List / Magnum Photos (PARI84694).

Page 120: Jed Fielding, *Naples, 1992.* © Jed Fielding.

Page 122: Herbert List, *Naples, 1958.* "Hearse on the promenade in front of the Fountain of Santa Lucia." © Herbert List / Magnum Photos (PARI84688).